POP CULTURE

American Life and Communication from the Telephone to Twitter

CATHLEEN SMALL

Cavendish Square
New York

Published in 2017 by Cavendish Square Publishing, LLC
243 5th Avenue, Suite 136, New York, NY 10016

First Edition

CPSIA Compliance Information: Batch #CS16CSQ

Library of Congress Cataloging-in-Publication Data

Names: Small, Cathleen, author.
Title: American life and communication from the telephone to Twitter / Cathleen Small.
Description: New York : Cavendish Square Publishing, 2017. |
Series: Pop culture | Includes bibliographical references and index.
Identifiers: LCCN 2016006894 (print) | LCCN 2016007060 (ebook) |
ISBN 9781502619778 (library bound) | ISBN 9781502619785 (ebook)
Subjects: LCSH: Telecommunication--United States--History--Juvenile literature.
| United States--Social life and customs--Juvenile literature.
Classification: LCC TK5102.4 .S63 2017 (print) | LCC TK5102.4 (ebook) |
DDC 384.0973--dc23
LC record available at http://lccn.loc.gov/2016006894

Editorial Director: David McNamara
Editor: Kelly Spence
Copy Editor: Nathan Heidelberger
Art Director: Jeffrey Talbot
Designer: Jessica Nevins
Production Assistant: Karol Szymczuk
Photo Research: J8 Media

The photographs in this book are used by permission and through the courtesy of: FPG/Hulton Archive/Getty Images (B&W), Petar Chernaev/Getty Images (color), cover; SSPL/Getty Images, 4, 41, 56; H. Armstrong Roberts/ClassicStock/Getty Images, 8; Camerique/Archive Photos/Getty Images, 12; George Marks/Retrofile/Getty Images, 16; Ron Burton/Getty Images, 19; Harold Adler/Underwood Archives/Getty Images, 23; AP Images, 26; Image Broker/Alamy Stock Photo, 29; Steve Jurvetson (http://www.flickr.com/people/44124348109@N01) from Menlo Park, USA/File:ARPANET first router.jpg/Wikimedia Commons, 31; Waring Abbott/Michael Ochs Archives/Getty Images, 34; Giulio Fornasar/Alamy Stock Photo, 37; Sclozza at English Wikipedia/File:425tdd.JPG/Wikimedia Commons, 40; Rama & Musée Bolo/File:Apple II IMG 4213.jpg/Wikimedia Commons, 43; Lionel Cironneau/AP Images, 46; Florian Fuchs/File:Motorola BMD-Pager.jpg/Wikimedia Commons, 50; Tim Boyle/Bloomberg/Getty Images, 52; Dudley Wood Alamy Stock Photo, 54; AAApictures/iStock/Thinkstock.com, 58; Paul K. Buck/AFP/Getty Images, 62; Brad Barket/Getty Images, 66; Roslan Rahman/AFP/Getty Images, 68; Alex Tan/AFP/Getty Images, 70; Asif Islam/Shutterstock.com, 73; Twin Design/Shutterstock.com, 75; Spencer Platt/Getty Images, 78; JAMES NIELSEN/AFP/Getty Images, 80; Wachiwit/Shutterstock.com, 84; Vasin Lee/Shutterstock.com, 87; Coronado/Shutterstock.com, 89; Prathan Chorruangsak/Shutterstock.com, 91; Anna Jurkovska,/Shutterstock.com 93; George Dolgikh/ Shutterstock.com, 94.

Printed in the United States of America

Contents:

Though innovative for their time, the first telephones from the 1800s barely resemble the tiny cell phones of today.

Introduction

COMMUNICATION FORMS THE BACKBONE of American society—and connects people from all over the world. Without it, we would just be three hundred million people sharing the same soil, and seven billion people sharing one planet. Communication is how we connect with one another and how we form relationships. It's also how we share hopes, dreams, concerns, and ideas.

Communications technology is constantly evolving, with new devices and methods being developed all the time. At the beginnings of civilization, there were **hieroglyphs** and cave drawings and oral tradition. Then came books, and then letters and telegrams. Then the telephone revolutionized communication—suddenly, you could instantly speak with someone far away instead of waiting for a letter to be delivered.

But it didn't end there. Telephone technology further developed, making it easier and cheaper to call people. Technological advancements provided deaf people with better communications tools. Eventually, there were conference calls and video calls and Internet calling.

Communications also branched off into other areas. Computers became more and more a part of people's everyday lives. Shortly thereafter, the Internet followed, which provided another layer of connectivity for people. With the Internet as its platform, social media exploded, providing people with a wealth of new friends made online, as well as connections to family and friends near and far. And when smartphones were developed, all of these communications tools suddenly became available all the time, at our fingertips.

So what have these advances in technology meant for society? Some people say that we're "too connected" now—that we socialize more with our devices than we do with each other. But you could flip that idea and look at it another way: we're actually *more* connected to people than ever before because we have more tools at our disposal. In the 1950s, for example, it was typical for men to go off to work while their wives stayed home and tended the house. In general, women didn't speak to their husbands during the workday—they saw them when they got home at dinnertime and for a few hours before bed. That didn't leave a whole lot of time for communication. But now, with people texting and e-mailing and being constantly available on their mobile phones, we are more apt to contact our family and friends throughout the day to check in—even with just a quick hello via text, e-mail, or social media. So in a way, our "too connected" society has actually used these leaps in technology to become more personally connected to each other.

The events of the last sixty-some years have shaped technology, and have also been influenced by it. For example, the Internet was initially created for the needs of the Department of Defense and the government. It was much later that it became available to the general public for widespread use. On the flip side, technological developments such as televised news broadcasts and the Internet have allowed Americans to learn more about what's going on in the world—and to become more aware of the factors at play in our nation. The Vietnam War, for example, was called the "Living Room War" because Americans were so connected to it through their televisions.

Today, technology and society are more intertwined than ever before. They affect each other, and they are affected *by* each other. The field of communications is constantly evolving and driving us forward, having taken us out of our bubble and shaped our twenty-first century society.

The ideal 1950s family consisted of a working father, stay-at-home mother, and well-behaved children.

ONE

1950s:

The American Dream

THE 1950S WERE THE DECADE OF THE American Dream. These golden years followed on the heels of the **Great Depression** (1929–1939) and the horrors of World War II (1939–1945). After years of turmoil, Americans craved security, stability, and a return to happiness. Americans wanted—more than anything—normalcy, and so they strove to create it in the form of the American Dream.

To find their American Dream, men—some returning from war and others adjusting to the societal upheaval that resulted from the troops returning home—often chose to marry and move their wives out to the **suburbs**. There, they could raise their future families in a quiet place, away from the hustle and bustle of the cities. Men often commuted to work in the city, leaving their wives at home to care for the children and manage the household.

This was a difficult adjustment for some women. World War II had given many women opportunities to work outside of the home for the first time. Some women worked directly in war efforts—either overseas or on the home front—

and others filled jobs vacated by men who had left to fight. Either way, more women were working outside the home, and many of them found they quite enjoyed it.

Returning to being homemakers and moving out to the suburbs wasn't exactly every woman's cup of tea. Some women, of course, craved that return to the normalcy they had grown up with. But others had gotten a taste of life outside the home, and they liked it. So, under the veneer of living out the American Dream in the suburbs, there lay a quiet unrest—a shifting of priorities and a struggle for both men and women to come to terms with changing gender roles.

The underlying unrest wasn't reserved to the suburbs. Even though World War II had ended, there was still conflict taking place in the world. The Korean War took place during the first three years of the decade, and the United States was uneasily involved. While Americans were concerned about the situation and wanted to help, they were also worried that any involvement in South Korea would add fire to growing tensions between the United States and the Soviet Union.

THE COLD WAR

The 1950s also marked the beginning of the **Cold War**, which put the United States and the Soviet Union at odds and left the looming threat of nuclear war hanging between the two. Both sides had nuclear weapons that could ensure destruction, and it was only by a tense agreement between the two that they were never deployed.

The Soviet Union was a communist nation. Fears about **communism** led to a "Red Scare" in the United States. One prominent face of this time was Republican Senator Joe McCarthy, who sought to find and prosecute suspected communists. While he primarily targeted people in the government and entertainment industry, he also accused teachers and people associated with labor unions of communist behavior. McCarthy's efforts, known as McCarthyism, resulted in the **blacklisting** of many big names in Hollywood in the late 1940s and early 1950s, including screenwriter Dalton Trumbo and actors Charlie Chaplin, Orson Welles, and Lloyd Bridges. McCarthy was far from alone in his efforts to weed out communists—the head of the Federal Bureau of Investigation (FBI), J. Edgar Hoover, was equally determined in his efforts to track down communists on US soil. In an interview published in the August 11, 1950 issue of *U.S. News & World Report*, he said: "We are interested in identifying ... every member of this international conspiracy in our midst, because every communist is a potential saboteur and espionage agent."

So while the 1950s were in some ways the decade of the American Dream, they were also a decade clouded by whispers of communism and the looming threat of nuclear war.

THE TELEVISION AS A COMMUNICATIONS DEVICE

The television was actually invented in the 1920s. There were some televised programs in the late 1930s and early 1940s, and the Radio Corporation of America (RCA), an electronics company, began to sell television sets during that same period. But televisions were still very new, and very few people had access to them. Also, the programming available was extremely limited. It wasn't until the late 1940s that commercial television broadcasting really began to spread across the United States. During the last few years of the 1940s, the number of television sets in American homes grew from about six thousand to about twelve million. The boom continued, with half of American households owning a television set by 1955.

This boom in television viewing and programming didn't help Senator McCarthy in his goal of exposing and prosecuting suspected communists. CBS news broadcaster

As more American families purchased TV sets in the 1950s, viewing became a family activity.

Edward R. Murrow broadcast a 1954 report that exposed McCarthy's questionable tactics in identifying and questioning these supposed communists. McCarthy tried to fight back in a TV appearance of his own, in which he accused Murrow himself of being a communist, but it was no use. The damage had been done, and Murrow supported his earlier assertions about McCarthy's questionable tactics by reiterating: "His proposition is very simple: anyone who criticizes or opposes McCarthy's methods must be a communist. And if that be true, there are an awful lot of communists in this country." Murrow's report was thought to be the beginning of the end of the McCarthy era. So important was Murrow's contribution to ending the reign of fear that existed with McCarthyism that George Clooney later directed a 2005 film about Murrow's efforts, entitled *Good Night, and Good Luck*—the line that Murrow used to sign off after his evening broadcasts.

News journalists like Murrow helped make television an important communications device of the 1950s. Before that time, Americans got most of their news from the newspaper or radio. But once televisions became commonplace in American homes, programs started to cover politics and other important news events as well. Walter Cronkite, who covered the presidential elections in 1952 for CBS, established the idea of a news anchorman. Shows like *The Huntley-Brinkley Report*, which debuted on the National Broadcasting Company (NBC) in 1956, brought the nightly news into American households.

Television technology was advancing in the 1950s, too. All television programs were broadcast in black and white until 1950, when a National Television System Committee was formed to help bring color to the TV screen, among other goals.

Television wasn't all about news and technological developments in the 1950s, though. It was also about fun and entertainment. One of the most popular shows on television in the 1950s was *I Love Lucy,* a **sitcom** starring Lucille Ball and her real-life husband, Desi Arnaz, as a married couple. *Lucy* was funny and entertaining, but it also made a subtle but pointed statement about **feminism**. On the show, Lucy was supposed to be a housewife, with her husband Ricky Ricardo acting as the breadwinner. In different episodes, Lucy is forever challenging that housewife role in a desire for more—in a subtle, humorous way. Audiences knew that Lucy and Ricky were real-life couple Lucille Ball and Desi Arnaz—a cross-cultural couple, with children, who were equal partners in their business enterprise. In its own humorous way, *I Love Lucy* showed viewers that women didn't have to be content as simply housewives, and that cross-cultural relationships, which were largely **taboo** in that era, were a possibility.

But there were certainly still television programs that enforced the idea of the traditional American family in the 1950s. *The Adventures of Ozzie and Harriet,* loosely based on the lives of the musical Nelson family, was wildly popular and held firm to 1950s values. The same held true for other popular shows of the decade, such as *Father Knows Best* and *Leave It to Beaver*.

As the 1950s went on, whatever viewers were looking for could increasingly be found on television. If they wanted news, it was there. If they wanted feel-good 1950s values-based programming, it was there. If they wanted something that challenged established norms a bit more, it was there, too. And so, television became an increasingly important and popular communications device as the decade rolled on.

TELEPHONY

The telephone was invented long before the 1950s, but it was still an incredibly relevant communications device in 1950s America. Not all homes had telephones, though. By 1946, telephones were in half of all American homes, but these homes were mostly in or near cities. People living in more rural areas still didn't often have telephones. However, the Rural Electrification Administration, authorized by Congress in 1949, sought to expand telephone coverage into rural and suburban areas. So, as the 1950s progressed, more and more people had telephones installed in their homes.

Interestingly, people in the 1950s didn't own their telephones. Instead, they rented them from AT&T, which held a monopoly on the telephone business for much of the twentieth century. Also, the technology behind telephone lines was different in the early 1950s. Back then, human operators manned local **telephone exchanges**. If you wanted to make a call, you had to have the operator place it for you. Direct dialing, which is what is used today, didn't come about until the 1950s. Neither did phone numbers as we currently know them. Up through the mid-1950s, phone numbers consisted of letters *and* numbers, with the letters being **mnemonics** that were names for the local telephone exchanges.

So, in the early 1950s, if you wanted to make a call, you asked the operator to place a call to, say, MU 5-9975, which stood for Murray Hill 5-9975—the phone number for Lucy and Ricky Ricardo's apartment in the *I Love Lucy* show!

As the population in the United States grew and as more homes had telephones installed, telephone company executives and engineers knew that they needed to find a better system. There weren't going to be enough working women to fill the

BC
EF
HI
KL
MNO
PRS
TUV
WXY
OPTR
1 2 3 4 5 6 7 8 9 0

Area Code Wars

The all-number system was slowly rolled out by Bell Labs in the 1950s, though it wasn't fully implemented until the 1960s. The new system resulted in a minor class war, where people took pride in living in supposedly desirable area codes. For example, San Francisco, long known as an extremely wealthy city, has the area code 415, and for a long time, people with that area code took a certain pride in it. That class war has diminished now that more and more people have cell phones instead of landline technology (and thus have the area code of where they bought the cell phone, not necessarily the area code of where they live), but for several decades, it was a sign of prestige to have a desirable area code.

demand for operators, which was strictly a woman's job in 1950s America. Also, the letter system sometimes resulted in misunderstandings and misplaced calls. They needed to move to an all-number system, and they needed to refine the technology for direct dialing and eliminate the need for live operators to place every call.

This move in technology was naturally met with some resistance—as many shifts in technology are. Some people felt that these changes were dehumanizing telephone communication. Much like arguments today that suggest texting will be the downfall of human communication, back in the 1950s, people argued that direct dialing would be the downfall of human communication! But ultimately, the United States moved to the direct dial, all-number system that we use today—and somehow, human communication survived.

***Opposite*: A 1950s-era direct-dial rotary telephone.**

In whichever system—telephone exchange or direct dial—telephones allowed Americans to keep each other up to date on the details of their lives. In the 1950s, with more families moving out to the suburbs, the phone was a way for extended families to keep in touch. It wasn't quite as easy as it is today, though. For one thing, telephones were strictly corded landlines—there were no cordless phones, and mobile technology had not yet been invented. Most households had only one phone line, so people had to share with the other members of their household. There was also no call-waiting, so if a call came in while someone was already talking on the phone, the caller simply got a busy signal and had to keep trying until the line was free.

Privacy was somewhat nonexistent, too. Most families had their telephone in a common area, such as the hallway or the family room, and because phones were corded, people couldn't disappear to another room when they wanted privacy. The solution for many teens wanting to have a private conversation with a boyfriend or girlfriend was to take the phone receiver, stretch out the long cord, and disappear into a hall closet for a whispered conversation.

If a family *did* have more than one phone in the house, they were generally all on the same phone line. Another family member could simply pick up the receiver of another extension in the house and listen in on the call.

Further, long-distance calls were expensive. When telephone service was strictly landlines, people had to pay long-distance charges to make calls outside of their area code. Rates were higher during the day than in the evenings and on weekends, so it wasn't as simple as picking up the phone whenever you wanted to call your boyfriend who was spending the summer across the country with his grandmother. Unless your family was relatively free with their money, you had to

Carbon No More! The Invention of the Copy Machine

Another communications device that made its debut in the 1950s was the copy machine. The technology for this device was actually invented in 1938, by an inventor named Chester Carlson who was experimenting in an apartment in Queens, New York. But the technology didn't make its public debut until about twenty years later, when Xerox released the model 914 copy machine. It was huge, heavy, and a fire hazard, but it revolutionized offices. Previously, secretaries had to make duplicate documents by using **carbon paper**, which was messy to use. Even with its slow copy rate of seven copies per minute, the Xerox 914 was a huge timesaver for secretaries. Now they could simply push a button and wait for the selected number of copies to appear.

The copy machine was so popular that Xerox, who introduced the machine to the public, became another name for the copy machine. Even machines produced by other companies are often informally called "Xerox machines." The word "xerox" was coined as a verb in 1965, with executives asking secretaries to "go xerox this, please."

An early duplicating machine was operated by hand to make several copies of a document.

wait until the rates dropped in the evening to make your call. Long-distance calling was *not* inexpensive in this era. People carefully chose when to make their phone calls and were mindful not to spend too long on the phone, or else they would receive a high bill for the call.

Still, with all of its drawbacks and challenges, the telephone system in the 1950s was a powerful communications tool. It was certainly much quicker and easier than sending letters, and people could hear the voices of their friends and loved ones, rather than simply imagining them as they read written letters.

DECADE IN REVIEW

The 1950s was a decade of superficial calm and deeper-running concerns over war and communism, but communications tools such as telephones and televisions allowed people to become more connected to each other than in previous decades. The television presented access to knowledge about what was going on in the world, and telephones allowed people to easily talk about their personal lives and global events. Even though families were separating as people moved out to the suburbs, in some ways they were closer than ever.

TWO

1960s: Peace, Love, and Unrest

THE COLD WAR DIDN'T END WITH THE 1950S. In fact, tensions were greater than ever in the early 1960s—and there would be a continued strain on relations between the United States and the Soviet Union for another thirty years. President John F. Kennedy took office in 1961 and shortly thereafter authorized the Bay of Pigs invasion of Cuba, intended to unseat dictator Fidel Castro. The United States government didn't trust Castro because of his alliance with Soviet leader Nikita Khrushchev. The invasion, though, was a dismal failure and further strained US relations with Cuba.

Indeed, Kennedy and his administration were probably right to be concerned about Castro's relationship with Khrushchev. The following year, they received intelligence that Cuba was allowing the Soviet Union to build nuclear missile sites on their land. Kennedy and Khrushchev were able to come to a tenuous agreement that resulted in the Soviet Union dismantling the missile sites. But tensions still ran high as Americans knew that their greatest enemy at that time had managed to build weapons of mass destruction dangerously close to US soil.

Meanwhile, another threat loomed over the heads of Americans—the war in Vietnam. Technically, the Vietnam War began in the 1950s and lasted until the 1970s, but much of the tension and unrest regarding the war took place in the 1960s. By this time, most American homes had television sets, and viewers were watching the so-called Living Room War unfold before them in full-color broadcasts. They didn't like what they saw.

First, there was the sheer brutality of the imagery they saw on the news—war is ugly, and for the first time, people at home could see parts of it right in front of them. But second, people also saw how the media could mold news based on bias and influence. Early during the American involvement in the war, the government had reported much success in the efforts to help South Vietnam triumph over North Vietnam. But thanks to **photojournalism** and news broadcasts, Americans eventually learned that some of these successes had been overinflated. There really wasn't much headway being made. Essentially, the US government was sending troops over to help South Vietnam, and soldiers were being killed without much, if any, gain for their efforts.

This created a feeling of disillusionment about American involvement in the war. Many people thought it was senseless for the United States to send troops to Vietnam when there was a great likelihood of them getting slaughtered. And they felt it wasn't even America's war—the conflict was between North and South Vietnam, so why was the United States bothering to get involved?

Opposite: Hippies were a sign of the 1960s counterculture and were fixtures at marches protesting the Vietnam War.

U-HAUL

The answer was related to the Cold War—the United States government feared that if communist North Vietnam were to triumph over South Vietnam, it would further the spread of communism in the world. This could ultimately be dangerous for the United States. And so, for a very long time, the government continued to send support to South Vietnam in the hopes that they would win the war, even when it became a losing battle.

Although the issue started with the Kennedy administration, President Lyndon B. Johnson shouldered much of the blame. Kennedy was a very popular president, and his untimely death by assassination only made him *more* popular. The American people had an image of the Kennedy presidency as a time of "Camelot"—a fanciful era of prosperity and hope. When Kennedy died, Camelot ended, and Vice President Johnson took office and inherited a whole lot of war issues and discontent.

As a result of American disillusionment with the Vietnam War and the government in general, **counterculture** arose. Counterculture simply refers to a group of people whose values and behaviors are different from those of mainstream society. There have been numerous examples of counterculture in history, but the counterculture of the 1960s is particularly well known because of how widespread it was—not only in the United States, but around the world, too.

The counterculture of the 1960s included so-called **hippies** and was concerned with peace, civil rights, feminism, sexual freedom, and experimentation with mind-altering drugs.

In short, the 1960s presented an America at odds with itself. On one side were those who clung to the 1950s ideal of the American Dream and the **patriarchal** household and supported US involvement in the Vietnam War. On the other side were people who opposed the war and embraced the idea of freedom and opportunity for all.

OFFICE COMMUNICATIONS

In the 1960s, most business offices were run under a patriarchal system where men held executive positions and women supported them as secretaries. The recent television series *Mad Men* depicts these roles in the advertising firm of Sterling Cooper, which is run like many such white-collar offices. There were still the telephone operators directing calls at the company switchboard, and there were still secretaries in the typing pool, typing up documents.

Typing grew significantly easier with the introduction of the IBM Selectric typewriter, introduced in 1961. Prior to the Selectric, typewriters were made of a set of typebars—one for each letter—that swung up to strike the paper through an ink ribbon when pressed. The problem with these typebars was that they frequently jammed, particularly if the typist accidently pressed two keys at once. With proficient typists churning out eighty to one hundred words per minute, you can imagine how easy it was to press two keys at once as your fingers flew over the keyboard.

The Selectric solved this problem by trading the "basket" of typebars in for a small typeball—literally a metal ball that had all of the letters on it. The ball rotated into position as letter keys were pressed, then placed the letter on the paper. Because of the technology that enabled the typeball to work, it was literally impossible for two letters to be pressed at once—it simply couldn't happen. Voila—the problem of jams was solved!

The typeball system was actually faster and more efficient than the basket of typebars, too, so secretaries could be more

A 1960s IBM Selectric, with its signature typeball on display

productive. Also, they could produce more professional-looking communications because the typeballs could easily be swapped out for those containing different fonts. So, for the first time, secretaries could essentially do desktop publishing, complete with multiple fonts in a single document.

Interestingly, as well as the series *Mad Men* depicted a typical 1960s white-collar office, it was *not* accurate in its portrayal of the typewriters used. Series creator Matthew Weiner admitted that he used Selectric II typewriters for the set, even though they weren't manufactured until 1971, for aesthetic reasons.

The offices of the 1960s were further made more efficient as photocopiers began to replace the old mimeograph machines that had been used for duplication. Documents produced by mimeograph had unmistakable purple text and released a pungent smell immediately after being produced. The type also wasn't as clear on mimeographs as it was on documents produced by a Xerox machine or other copier. Making carbon copies while typing was another option if only two copies of a document were required, but the resulting copy wasn't terribly clear, either.

The Xerox was introduced in the late 1950s, and throughout the 1960s, more and more offices retired their old mimeograph machines and carbon paper in favor of the new Xerox technology, making secretaries' jobs far easier and more efficient.

Never content to sit back and relax, Xerox continued to innovate in the 1960s by producing the first fax machines. People had been playing with fax technology for a while, but no one had yet invented what we have come to know as the fax machine until Xerox released the LDX (short for Long-Distance Xerography) in 1964. Its successor, the Magnafax 840, debuted in 1966. The LDX was actually a commercial flop (largely due to its high price tag), but the Magnafax—which was developed by Magnavox but marketed by Xerox—was a success.

FAMILY COMMUNICATIONS

Although counterculture was going strong in the 1960s, the American family was still equally strong. There were those members of society who chose to distance themselves from their family structure and live a more **nomadic**, hippie existence, but there were certainly also people who continued to value a more traditional family structure. The communications devices of the 1960s mirrored that.

Television was still a huge communications medium. At the beginning of the decade, nearly nine out of ten American households had a television set, and television viewing was up to an average of five hours per day per household. Because most families at that time had only one television set, TV viewing was a communal activity where the family gathered around the set.

News programs were very popular, given the current affairs of the time—wars, presidential elections, assassinations—but families also gathered to watch sitcoms and other television shows, such as *The Andy Griffith Show*, *The Dick Van Dyke Show*, and *Bonanza*. Watching television together provided families with a common, shared interest.

Interestingly, the counterculture was not left out of this family experience. In the mid-1960s, television programming slowly began to evolve from depicting the American Dream and nuclear families to showing different types of families, such as one-parent households (*Bonanza* and *My Three Sons*) and unusual households (*The Addams Family*, *The Munsters*, and *Bewitched*). There was still a lot of taboo in television (for example, in the late 1960s and early 1970s, the married

Family Memories: The Carousel

One popular item during this era was the slide projector. Families would take pictures while on vacation or around family events and have them developed into slides, which they could then project on the wall in a slideshow. People liked to good-naturedly groan as old Uncle Joe once again hauled out slides from the family's vacation to the seashore. But in reality, these slideshows were another time of family bonding—a chance to remember times spent together or family members and friends no longer living.

In 1961, Kodak introduced the revolutionary carousel project. It held eighty slides loaded into a round "carousel," and it allowed for mostly jam-free slideshows that didn't require the person showing the slides to manually reset the tray. The carousel made it far easier for old Uncle Joe to hold his slideshows—to the delight and chagrin of family members everywhere!

The Kodak Carousel slide projector.

couple in *The Brady Bunch* were not allowed to be shown sharing a bed—they had to be shown in separate beds), but the media was slowly moving to portray a range of lifestyles.

THE BEGINNINGS OF THE INTERNET

The Cold War was actually part of the inspiration for a major development in communications technology that would eventually contribute to the Internet. In the event of a weapons strike by the Soviet Union, the government knew that the president would need to be able to quickly make a series of decisions and communications. These decisions would need to be transmitted quickly and without relying on a central communications hub—the technology being used at that point in time.

The problem was that if a central communications hub was destroyed by a missile strike, then the president's directives could not be sent. So, they needed a system that could address that potential problem. A researcher for the think tank RAND came up with a solution that involved data being broken into "packets" and traveling along a network of nodes with no central hub. This complicated technology, known as packet switching, combined analog communications technology and digital computer technology. It eventually formed the basis of what would later be the Internet. At the time, though, it was simply a way to ensure that any strikes associated with the Cold War would not disable communications in the United States.

***Opposite*: Much like old telephones, computers from several decades ago were much larger than their counterparts today!**

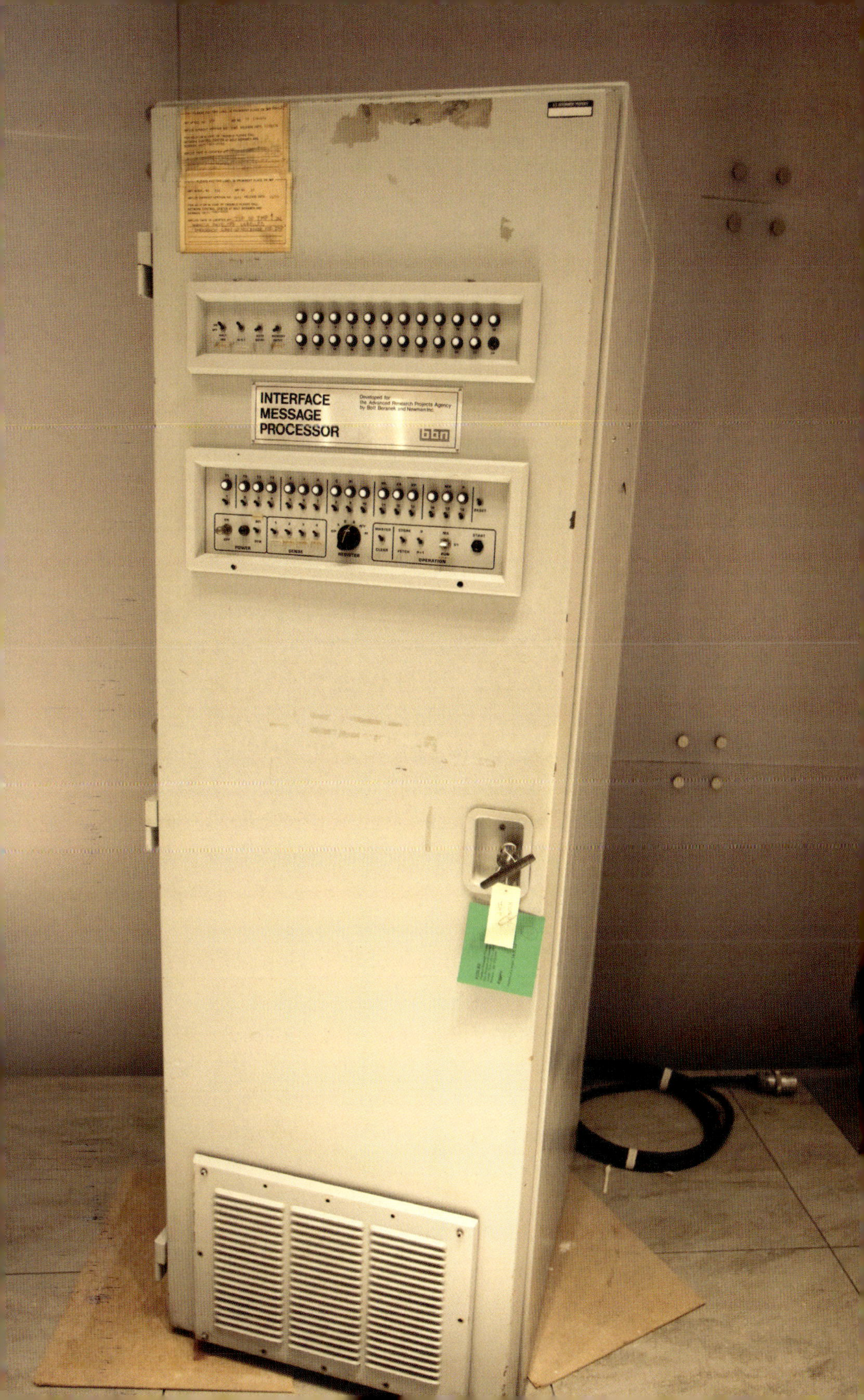
INTERFACE
MESSAGE
PROCESSOR
Developed for
the Advanced Research Projects Agency
by Bolt Beranek and Newman Inc.
bbn

Another related technology developed later in the 1960s was the Advanced Research Projects Agency Network (ARPANET), the precursor to the modern World Wide Web and e-mail. ARPANET was further developed in the early 1970s, but its beginnings were rooted in the late 1960s, when the Department of Defense determined a way to move data files between data processing sites at universities and military bases. It existed in the mind of one J. C. R. Licklider from MIT even earlier, though, when he described a "galactic network" concept in 1962. Once ARPANET was up and running, it quickly developed into the first e-mail system and eventually the World Wide Web.

Numerous researchers were working on technologies related to packet switching and ARPANET at the same time. Eventually, that technology combined to become ARPANET and later the World Wide Web and Internet. So this technology, which would later completely restructure the entire way we communicate, was never the brainchild of one or two people. It was the result of many people working on similar, complementary technologies that eventually came together to form the communications system we have today.

DECADE IN REVIEW

The 1960s was a time of division in the United States—those who supported the war efforts and those who were against them, and those who clung to the American Dream and those who embraced the counterculture. Through it all, communications devices supported both worlds. New technologies in office communications made the lives of working females easier. The continuing rise in the popularity of television offered choices that appealed to many. And amid all the chaos, the seeds of the Internet were being planted and were starting to sprout.

THREE

1970s: Watergate, Women's Rights, and the "Me Decade"

AS THE 1960S TURNED INTO THE 1970S, THE United States was still heavily involved in the Vietnam War, much to the displeasure of many Americans—in particular, members of the counterculture movement. Some Americans still harbored a distrust of the government, which only worsened when the Watergate scandal broke in the early part of the decade.

The Watergate scandal started with a June 1972 break-in at the Democratic National Committee headquarters (which were located in an office complex called Watergate, thus the name of the political scandal). It was later determined that President Richard Nixon, a Republican, likely had something to do with the break-in—or at the very least, his staff did. Investigations also uncovered multiple other unethical activities undertaken by the Nixon administration, of which the president himself had knowledge and helped to cover up. These incidents included secretly taping conversations, bugging the offices

Carl Bernstein (*left*) and Robert Woodward (*right*) broke the Watergate scandal for the *Washington Post*.

of political rivals, and harassing other political figures and members of activist groups. Nixon initially claimed that he had no part in any wrongdoing, saying to the press: "I am not a crook," and "I want the facts out, because the facts will prove that the president is telling the truth." However, when the US Supreme Court ruled that President Nixon had to turn over the tapes of the conversations he had recorded in his office, the president's attempts to cover up illegal and unethical activities were revealed. Nixon resigned in August 1974 when it became clear that he would be impeached.

Naturally, the public's confidence in the presidential administration was shaken. Political corruption was nothing new, but rarely was it put on full display as it was during the Watergate scandal. It did, however, produce a couple of unlikely heroes—*Washington Post* reporters Robert Woodward and Carl Bernstein, who covered the Watergate scandal. Woodward and Bernstein's reporting on the scandal earned the paper a Pulitzer Prize for Public Service, and they later turned their notes and reporting into a book called *All the President's Men*. The book was a major success for the publishing industry and was later adapted into a movie starring Robert Redford and Dustin Hoffman. Woodward and Bernstein became legends in the world of news reporting after their coverage of the scandal. To this day, their work continues to set a standard for journalistic excellence.

While the men in high-ranking government positions were trying to do damage control against the Watergate scandal and the strong antiwar sentiment, women in America were fighting their own battle for equal rights. Feminism had been gaining strength throughout the 1960s, and a post-war employment boom meant that more women were in the workforce. However, women were still largely relegated to secretarial roles and had to work for much lower salaries than men. *Roe v. Wade,* the

1973 Supreme Court decision that legalized first-trimester abortions, was a pivotal moment in the feminist movement. Later in the 1970s, the movement began to shine light on physical and sexual abuse of women with events such as annual Take Back the Night marches.

Women were gaining more rights in the 1970s and thus more confidence in themselves, but that consciousness of self was not limited to females. The 1970s in general were considered the "me decade," a phrase coined by author Tom Wolfe. Wolfe meant that Americans in the 1970s were focused very much on themselves, with little thought to how their actions affected the community around them. With that focus on "me" naturally came an interest in what sorts of devices could make one's life easier.

CUTTING THE CORD: CORDLESS AND MOBILE PHONES

The telephone had been a major communications device for Americans for decades, but they were stationary, attached to the wall by a cord, so there was very little privacy. You could stretch the phone cord and disappear into the closet to have a chat, but that was the extent of it.

That changed in the 1970s, when cordless phones were introduced. The technology for cordless phones was actually invented in 1965, by jazz musician Teri Pall, but it was unusable because it interfered with aircraft communication signals. Pall ended up selling her idea to a manufacturer a few years later. The manufacturer modified the technology so it wouldn't

***Opposite*: An early cordless phone handset.**

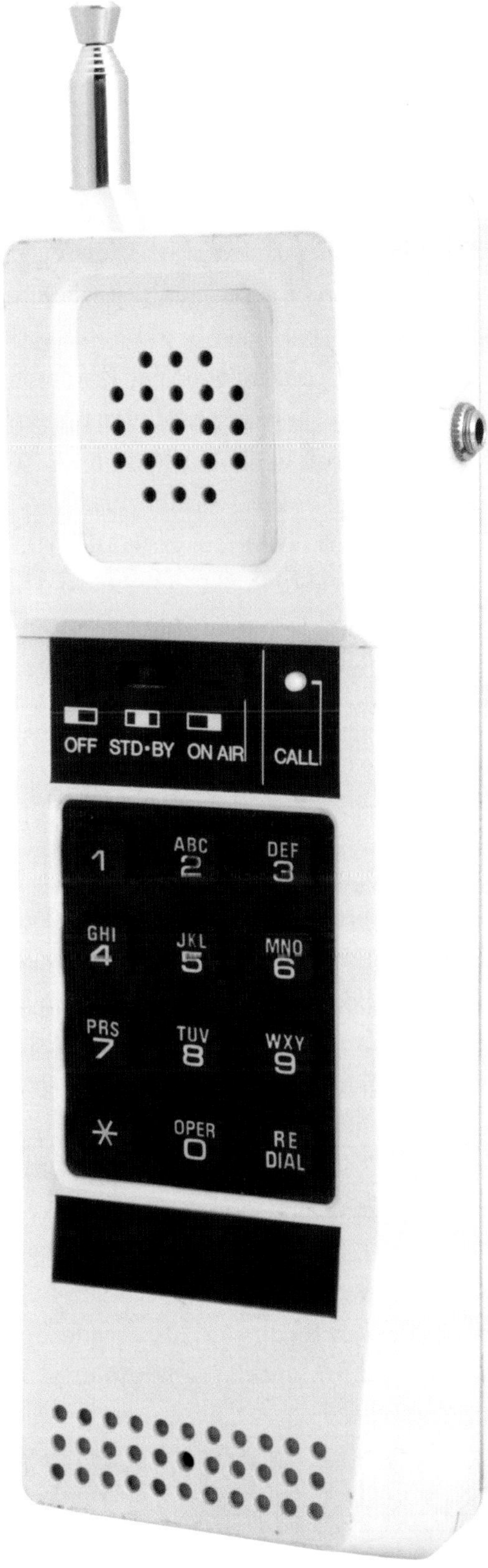
OFF
STD•BY
ON AIR
CALL
1
ABC 2
DEF 3
GHI 4
JKL 5
MNO 6
PRS 7
TUV 8
WXY 9
*
OPER 0
RE DIAL

interfere with aircraft communication and later marketed cordless phones to the public.

Like all new technology, cordless phones were very expensive at first. They didn't start showing up in homes until the late 1970s and early 1980s. But when they did, they were revolutionary—particularly to people seeking privacy on their phone calls! Suddenly, you could wander around the house with the phone—sometimes even outside.

Still, though, cordless phones had limits. You had to be in or very close to the house. Cordless phones weren't *mobile* phones—you couldn't take them on a quick run to the store with you. Well, you could if you were Dr. Martin Cooper of Motorola—the first person to make a call on a mobile phone. Cooper, the inventor of the first personal mobile phone, made this historic call in 1973. This was two years after AT&T first proposed the mobile-phone system as it exists today—technology dividing cities into series of "cells" for the purposes of calling.

After a few years of legal wrangling over monopolies, cell-phone development began in earnest in 1977, when the Federal Communications Commission allowed Bell Telephone Company and AT&T to begin cell testing in Chicago. But widespread cell-phone use didn't begin until the late 1990s. Before that, cell phones were *extremely* expensive, and the cell network was still in development.

Nowadays, it's hard to imagine being without our cell phones—people can reach us virtually anywhere at any time. But back in the 1970s, you had to be home to get a call. And if you weren't … well, you just missed the call. Answering machines were invented during this decade, but not widely owned. They wouldn't become common until the 1980s.

TELECOMMUNICATIONS FOR THE DEAF COMMUNITY

In the mid-to-late 1960s, two deaf men, James Marsters and Robert Weitbrecht, began working on technology to develop the **teletypewriter** (TTY), a telecommunications device for the deaf (sometimes also known as a TDD).

Deaf people had long communicated with sign language, but naturally that didn't translate to telephone communication. Marsters and Weitbrecht partnered with Andrew Saks (from the family who founded the Saks Fifth Avenue chain of department stores) and founded the Applied Communications Corporation, also known as APCOM. Basically, APCOM worked to develop a modem of sorts, which they attached to discarded teleprinter machines (communications ports for mainframe computers). The resulting device was then hooked up to a touch-tone phone, and the entire unit was able to send and receive messages.

Like most technology, the initial device was primitive, allowing only one-way communication, but it laid the foundation on which future TTY devices were built. At a 1973 convention for the deaf in California, the Manual Communications Module (MCM) was introduced by Micon Industries. It met with instant popularity, in part because it was the first such device to allow two-way communication. Micon later teamed with APCOM, and the MCMs began to be distributed to the hearing-impaired community free of charge.

TDDs revolutionized communication for the deaf. No longer did deaf people need to be face to face with another person to communicate, or write letters that wouldn't be received for days. In cases where a deaf person wanted to use the phone to call a person who was able to hear, they could

An early TTY/TDD device.

use their TTY to call a telecommunications relay service (or TRS). The person could enter their speech on the TDD, and the relay operator would then verbally relay the message to the person on the other end of the call. When that person responded, the relay operator would use a TDD to relay the response back to the deaf caller.

It wasn't a perfect system, but it was certainly a massive improvement. One of the most exciting parts about the evolution of communications technology is how it has enabled people who previously couldn't communicate to have a voice—because even people who can't speak have something to say.

VHS or Betamax?

An exciting development in the mid-1970s was the commercial release of the videocassette recorder, or VCR. These devices allowed people to record television shows and play them back, or to rent or buy movies on videocassette. As often happens, though, there were a couple of related, competing technologies released around the same time. JVC released the Video Home System (or VHS) format, and Sony released the Betamax format. VHS tapes couldn't play on Betamax machines, and vice versa—so you either went with one or the other. The technologies were similar, but Betamax offered slightly higher quality and a slightly shorter recording time.

In the end, the decision for most people came down to price. The VHS was cheaper than Betamax and consumers couldn't really tell the difference in picture quality, so they opted for the less expensive option. And so, VHS won the videotape war over Betamax.

A Betamax machine.

LEAPS IN PERSONAL COMPUTING

Although the seeds of the Internet were planted in the 1960s, they really began to sprout and bear fruit in the 1970s. ARPANET was formally introduced in the early 1970s, along with its capability for e-mail transmission. It was revolutionary, but computer scientists quickly realized its limitations—it was a closed system, and something more open was needed.

Enter TCP/IP, which stands for Transmission Control **Protocol**/Internet Protocol, a technology still in use today. TCP/IP was basically a different networking protocol that enabled multiple networks to be connected together but also stand alone. The networks worked together, but they were all individual so that if one network collapsed, the others would not be affected. The TCP/IP was so successful that the Internet as we know it today was eventually built on the protocol.

Meanwhile, at Xerox, researchers were working on data-transmission networks that would allow much quicker transfer of data in much larger packages than radio transmission had previously allowed—an integral component for what would later become the Internet.

All of this pre-Internet technology was exciting for researchers and scientists, but it didn't necessarily mean much to the average Joe or Jane—yet. What *did* catch the attention of the average American was the personal computer (PC), which was introduced in the 1970s. Once the "me generation" got wind of this new technology and the idea of personal computing, they were intrigued. Computers were expensive, but oh so handy. In particular, the word-processing features

***Opposite*: The Apple II was wildly popular with consumers, thanks in part to its easy-to-use operating system.**

IN USE
DRIVE 2
disk II
IN USE
DRIVE 1
disk II
apple II

of personal computers made producing documents infinitely easier—no more using whiteout to correct mistakes in typing!

The first personal computers, produced by Commodore, Tandy, and others, were wildly expensive and impractical for home use. Commodore produced the PET in 1977, which was marketed as a personal computer, and Tandy introduced the TRS-80. The TRS-80 was relatively affordable and came fully assembled with a monitor, a keyboard, and audiocassette storage. It also featured the BASIC software. These models, although successful, had a sneaky competitor lurking in the background: the Apple II.

The Apple II was similar to the TRS-80 in that it used the BASIC language and had a self-contained keyboard. But it used a television for the display, and instead of audiocassette storage it relied on a floppy disk drive. The Apple II had the added bonus of offering a spreadsheet program called VisiCalc that appealed to many users.

In a stroke of marketing brilliance, Apple Computer focused their marketing efforts on schools. Students learned how to use the computers at school and then wanted the same type of computer at home. As far as personal computers of the time went, the Apple models were relatively easy to learn and use. They made a logical first choice for many families venturing into the world of home computing.

Home computers wouldn't become commonplace until the 1980s, but the introduction of personal computers and the Apple II in the late 1970s set an exciting stage for things to come.

DECADE IN REVIEW

The 1970s started off in the turmoil of war and government corruption and eased into a "me generation" where women continued upward movement in society, making strides in employment and women's rights. Communications devices were become more appealing for personal use, with the emphasis on the portability of cordless phones and mobile phones and on the ease and flexibility that personal computers would provide.

As the 1970s came to a close, the United States was on the verge of an explosion in technology and communication—even if no one yet knew just how big that explosion would eventually be.

FOUR

1980s:

Walls Come Down, and an Epidemic Rises

WITH THE END OF THE 1970S "ME DECADE" came the 1980s—and naturally, more change. American culture is nothing if not forever changing!

In the 1980s, political relations were slowly warming with the Soviet Union. Mikhail Gorbachev was the leader of the Soviet Union from 1985 to 1991. Under his leadership and President Ronald Reagan's administration, the United States and the Soviet Union greatly repaired their political relationship, which eventually led to the end of the Cold War as the 1980s drew to a close.

A major event in the decline of the Cold War was the fall of the Berlin Wall. The wall had physically divided East (communist) and West (noncommunist) Berlin since 1961, but its gates were finally opened to all on November 9, 1989.

***Opposite*: The fall of the Berlin Wall marked a major shift at the end of the 1980s.**

That same day, physical demolition of the wall began. Less than a month later, the Cold War was officially over.

With the threat of war with the Soviet Union effectively over (and in fact the Soviet Union would cease to exist less than two years later), Americans had one worry off their plates. But they had another rising concern: the Middle East. **Islamism** was rising in the region, and with it certain **extremist groups**, including al-Qaeda. Although the Middle East was not on most Americans' radar as a threat back in the 1980s, the reality is that extremist groups from the region would later become a greater threat to America.

But many Americans lived in blissful ignorance about this for a while. Instead, they feared a very real threat on US soil: a disease known as AIDS. In 1981, reports began to pop up about homosexual males contracting and dying of an unusual **immunodeficiency disease**. By the end of the year, there were already 270 reported cases of the mysterious disease, and 121 people had died—all of them homosexual men.

News of AIDS spread, but for a time, many people assumed that only homosexual males were at risk. Then came the end of 1982 and reports of twenty-three infants diagnosed with an unexplained disease. At least one of these children was positively identified as having AIDS.

By early 1983, women were turning up with the disease, and the Centers for Disease Control (CDC) identified that the transmission of AIDS required an exchange of bodily fluids through sexual contact, blood transfusion, or intravenous drug use. Panic ensued when Americans learned of Ryan White, a thirteen-year-old boy diagnosed with HIV (the virus that causes AIDS), reportedly from a blood transfusion, and Kimberly Ann Bergalis, a woman who contracted the virus from her HIV-positive dentist.

Americans were in a panic. They knew not to share needles or have unprotected intercourse, but they didn't know whether simple contact, such as kissing or even hugging, could transmit HIV. The disease was awful, there was no cure, and no one could be certain just how contagious it was. It was a time of fear for many Americans.

But the 1980s was also an exciting decade. It was becoming easier and more affordable to connect and communicate while on the go. Corded phones were rapidly becoming a distant memory, and sleeker computers were replacing manual typewriters. Change was in the air, and it was exciting!

PAGE ME!

Pager technology was actually invented in the late 1940s, but it was reserved strictly for use by physicians. It was expensive, but the idea was that doctors could be reached for emergencies at any time through their pager. However, widespread pager use among the general public didn't occur until the late 1970s and the 1980s.

A pager was a small, portable device that the wearer could clip onto a belt or simply carry in a pocket or purse. When a call was made to a pager, the device would beep or vibrate to alert the receiver. Modern pagers had a screen that displayed the number of the incoming call, though for some pagers, the caller had to manually enter the phone number on a touch-tone phone for it to show up on the recipient's pager.

It seems like a rather primitive device by today's standards, but in the 1980s and early 1990s, pagers were exciting and quite useful. Many people didn't have cell phones, so if they didn't want to miss phone calls while on the go, the solution was a pager. It was small, relatively inexpensive, and reliable.

An early Motorola pager.

When a call came in, the recipient could simply find an available phone (pay phone or otherwise) and return the call. Simple!

Certainly doctors and other professionals used pagers during the 1980s, but they were also widely used by teenagers who didn't want to miss calls from friends! And just as there is now texting lingo, such as LOL (laugh out loud) and ROTFL (rolling on the floor laughing), there was also pager lingo. Because pagers generally took numbers (although some could receive text, in the 1980s, most teen-owned pagers simply took numbers), the pager-speak was in the form of numerical codes. If you wanted someone to call you back immediately, for example, you would enter 911 (the common phone number for emergencies). If you just wanted to ask what was going on, you would enter 411 (the common phone number for Information, which you would call if you couldn't find a phone number—Information is obsolete these days, but it used to be a lifeline when you didn't have Google to look up phone numbers!).

Pagers were a bit of a status symbol, too. Just as it's now somewhat unusual to find people who don't own a cell phone, back in the 1980s and 1990s all the cool, tech-savvy people owned pagers!

CELL PHONES

Ah, cell phones. They're everywhere today! Who doesn't have a cell phone? It's actually rather unusual to go to a public place and *not* see dozens of people with their cell phones out.

But back in the 1980s, cell phones were just starting to emerge among the general public. Motorola, the big name in pager manufacturing, also introduced one of the early cell phones: the DynaTAC 8000x. Introduced in 1983, it cost a whopping $3,995 (for reference, that would be nearly

MOTOROLA
Rcl
Clr
Sto
Fcn
End
Pwr
Lock
Vol

$10,000 in today's market), and it was *huge* compared to the sleek devices available now. It was, however, technically small enough to carry, so it was considered mobile.

Those who could only dream of owning such a piece of technology had to be content to drool over it when Gordon Gekko carried it in the movie *Wall Street* and Zack Morris used it in the TV series *Saved by the Bell*. For most people, though, the price tag was simply too high.

By the late 1980s, cell phones were becoming more portable and more like what we know them to be today. Motorola (again on the cutting edge of technology) introduced the MicroTAC phone in 1989. It was an early flip phone with a collapsible antenna, and it was actually designed to fit in a pocket—far more portable than the DynaTAC. It was still quite pricey, though, starting at $2,495 in 1989 dollars (roughly $5,000 today). This was out of the price range of many Americans, but still—cell-phone technology was improving and slowly becoming more affordable.

A New Type of Memory

Just as the 1970s had helped families share their memories with the technology of the carousel slide projector, the 1980s brought a new way to document special occasions: the camcorder.

Video cameras had been around for quite a while, naturally. News media outlets, for example, had been using them for decades, and some families had been able to record home movies before the 1980s, but they were the exception to

***Opposite*: The Motorola DynaTAC was one of the earliest mobile phones.**

An early camcorder and 1980s-era storage media.

the rule. Most families simply recorded their memories in still pictures.

But in 1983, Sony released the Betamovie BMC-100P, the first consumer camcorder. JVC, Panasonic, RCA, and Hitachi followed not far behind with models of their own. At first, these cameras were mostly used by amateur videographers and college television studios, but soon families began to buy camcorders to film home videos of their growing children. In fact, camcorders became so popular that there was even a television show devoted to people's home movies: *America's Funniest Home Videos*, which debuted in 1989.

At that time, there was no YouTube on which to share your videos, but at least you could watch them in your home and share them with your friends and family manually. Compared to the Polaroid snapshots and slideshows of the previous decades, it was quite an advancement.

PERSONAL COMPUTERS AND THE INTERNET CONTINUE TO GROW

The 1980s were a time of great development in personal computing and the Internet. The TCP/IP technology on which the Internet was built was developed in the 1970s, but it wasn't put into practical use until 1983, when it replaced ARPANET (although ARPANET was not fully decommissioned until 1990). In 1984, the domain name system (DNS) was launched, which led to the .com, .gov, and .org domains we all know and love.

By 1985, the Internet was in place and supporting some communities of researchers and businesses, although it wasn't anywhere near ready for casual home use at that point. E-mail, too, had been developed and was in use, but generally within

An IBM PC, circa 1981.

certain relatively small communities—it wasn't yet widespread and in use by the general public.

Meanwhile, in the personal computing world, IBM launched its first personal computer in 1981. In a rather surprising move, *Time* magazine decided its 1982 Man of the Year would be the computer. Apple Computer made headlines again when it launched the Macintosh on January 24, 1984. A handsome, young Steve Jobs introduced the revolutionary new computer—which was surprisingly small by 1980s standards—but then let it "speak for itself," and the mighty little machine announced to the crowd, "Hello. I'm Macintosh … Never trust a computer you can't lift!"

The Macintosh was groundbreaking in the world of home computers because it was incredibly user friendly, with a cheerful interface that greeted users with a smile upon booting up. Beyond the cheery smile, though, what made the Mac so user friendly was the graphical user interface (GUI) and mouse. Before the Mac, personal computers didn't use a GUI. There was no way to point and click because there was no mouse! Instead, users of other personal computers had to type in commands to perform the tasks they desired. That was all fine and good for people familiar with these types of commands, but it proved rather difficult for people unfamiliar with the operating system to learn.

But anyone could use the Mac! Once you learned how to point and click, you were off and running! It was pure genius. Equally brilliant was the advertisement used to introduced the Mac to the market: a Ridley Scott–directed masterpiece based on George Orwell's novel *Nineteen Eighty-Four* and broadcast in the most coveted of timeslots—during the Super Bowl.

The ad particularly appealed to people on the fringes or in the counterculture because of its subject matter. Orwell's novel *Nineteen Eighty-Four* is a story set in the future (in

Tiny but mighty: the user-friendly Mac!

this case, the year 1984) where people are controlled by Big Brother, a dictator of sorts whose regime watches everyone on telescreens. For members of the counterculture of the 1960s and 1970s, it was the worst possible scenario imaginable—a place where everyone was expected to conform at all times. There was no room for freedom of expression in Orwell's story.

In the Macintosh ad inspired by the book, droves of men, all dressed alike in drab gray clothing, march into a room where they are watching a speech about conformity by Big Brother, being shown on a large screen and many other small screens. A woman clad in red and white runs into the room amid the sea of drably clothed conformists and throws a hammer at the big screen, shattering the face of Big Brother and ending his message. The woman represents the invention of the new, different computer, poised to save civilization from conformity (a sea of PCs and IBM clones). Undoubtedly, the message was appealing to members of the counterculture, who desired individuality and expression—and even just to those people on the fringes, who aspired to be just a little bit different from the masses. The message was clear: step outside the box, and avoid falling into the drab world of PCs and IBMs.

Although the ad only ran on television twice (due to an issue with possible copyright infringement with George Orwell's estate), it was enough to get people's attention. It established Apple as the computer for those who wanted to stand apart from the rest. And indeed, Apple has continued that strategy—their 1997 "Think Different" slogan was widely believed to be a dig at rival IBM's "Think" motto. IBM was for the standard brainiacs, and Apple was for the gifted creative thinkers. To this day, people speak of the "Cult of Mac"—Mac users are a devoted bunch who remain true to the company and its products. They are fewer and farther between than PC

Super Bowl Ads: Instant Cultural Classics

It was a wise marketing decision for Apple to broadcast their 1984 Macintosh commercial during the Super Bowl. The Super Bowl is consistently among the year's most watched television programs, so naturally an advertising spot during such a highly viewed program would be coveted. However, Super Bowl ad spots have become even more valuable because the ads that air during the game have become sort of a cultural phenomenon. The ads are often introducing new products—such as the Macintosh in 1984—and often the companies who have paid for these highly sought-after spots have also paid dearly to have creative, inventive, and just plain cool ads filmed! Super Bowl ads have become so popular that many non-football fans watch the game *just* to see the ads!

In addition to Apple, Coca-Cola, Doritos, and Budweiser are among the well-known companies who have scored big with their Super Bowl ads. However, these ad spots don't come cheap—the average cost of a thirty-second ad spot during the 2015 Super Bowl was $4.5 million.

and Windows users, but they are passionately devoted. They are, perhaps, the counterculture of the home computing world.

But the problem with Macs in the 1980s was that they were expensive. For many people, a desktop PC such as an IBM clone or a Commodore 64 was far more affordable. And truly, not much has changed—you will *still* pay more for a Mac than you will for most PCs! Apple works on a theory that quality, service, and elegance don't come cheap, and that business model seems to have served them well since the introduction of their first computers.

DECADE IN REVIEW

From pagers to the Apple computer, by the close of the 1980s people were more connected than ever. New technologies increased awareness of events like the AIDS epidemic, and companies were dreaming up more user-friendly and affordable devices.

FIVE

1990s: Terrorism and New Media

THE END OF THE 1980S BROUGHT THE END of the Cold War, but that didn't mean the end of unrest in the world. There was widespread poverty in Africa, as well as political tensions and **genocide**. And in the European country of Yugoslavia, tensions between the Serbians and Croatians brought about genocide and civil war.

The United States largely stayed out of the conflicts in Africa and Yugoslavia but entered into a brewing conflict in the Middle East in the early part of the 1990s. Dictator Saddam Hussein was ruling Iraq and invaded Kuwait, at which point the United States sent troops into the Persian Gulf and entered into the Gulf War, a conflict that lasted several months in late 1990 and early 1991. This was the start of the US military presence in the Middle East, which continued throughout the decade.

Opposite: In an act of domestic terrorism, two American men blew up the Alfred P. Murrah Federal Building in Oklahoma City.

Meanwhile, further tensions with the Middle East were brewing. The Taliban and al-Qaeda continued to gain power, and in 1993 it became clear just what a threat they were, with a terrorist attack on the World Trade Center. The attack was largely unsuccessful—a bomb in the underground parking garage was meant to bring down both towers. It did, however, tragically kill six people and injure more than one thousand others—and it sent a very clear message to Americans about just how upset al-Qaeda was about US support of Israel, with whom they were in conflict. Not quite a decade later, of course, al-Qaeda would launch another attack against the United States and this time succeed in bringing down the Twin Towers.

But the Middle East wasn't the only threat to the United States—a fact proven when American-born Timothy McVeigh and Terry Nichols bombed the Alfred P. Murrah Federal Building in Oklahoma City in 1995. McVeigh and Nichols's attack killed 168 people and injured nearly 700 more—some of them children from a daycare center in the building. The attack was motivated by McVeigh and Nichols's dislike of the federal government.

Timothy McVeigh was a veteran of the Gulf War, but it wasn't the war that caused his dislike for the federal government. Instead, it was his displeasure for how a couple of domestic incidents were handled. One was the Waco, Texas, siege in which the FBI and the Bureau of Alcohol, Tobacco, Firearms and Explosives (ATF) raided a compound near Waco held by the Branch Davidians, a religious cult, in 1993. A total of eight-two Branch Davidians were killed in the siege, along with four ATF agents. The second incident was at Ruby Ridge, Idaho, where United States Marshals and the FBI killed two members of a family who were thought to be part of the Aryan Nation and involved in illegal weapons activities. A US marshal was also killed in the incident.

These terrorist incidents were not exactly unique—for as long as civilization has existed, there have been conflicts resulting in tragedy and death. But what made them so poignant for the American public was how much in the public eye they were. With television and the Internet continuing its wildfire spread, Americans now had access to information and news twenty-four hours a day, seven days a week, from a variety of sources—some reliable and some not so reliable. Because of that, more people were aware of the goings-on in the world—which was both a blessing and a curse. It brought awareness, certainly, but it also brought concern and sometimes misinformation.

Speculation and misinformation certainly flew around the Internet when another major event of the late 1990s broke into the public eye: the potential impeachment of President Bill Clinton, who admitted in 1998 to having an intimate relationship with a young White House intern named Monica Lewinsky. The general public watched and read in fascination as the scandal unfolded. Initially, the president denied any wrongdoing, but eventually he confessed to the affair and to lying about his involvement in it. While the supposed truth eventually came out, the television and Internet coverage abounded with theories and speculation. Such was the nature of media and information in the changing technical environment of the 1990s.

THE INTERNET CATCHES FIRE

As the 1990s opened, an era was coming to a close—ARPANET, the precursor to the World Wide Web, was officially decommissioned, and the World Wide Web

Who Invented the Internet?

While campaigning to secure the Democratic nomination for president in 1999, then–Vice President Al Gore supposedly claimed he invented the Internet. He was widely mocked for this statement, as it was well known this was not true. However, the incident was somewhat incorrectly reported—Gore never actually claimed he invented the Internet; rather, he stated that he "took the initiative in creating the Internet." He was likely referring to the fact that during his time in the United States Congress, he backed initiatives such as the High Performance Computing Act, which enabled researchers to continue developing Internet technology. It was confusing phrasing, to be sure, but it's a myth that he claimed to have invented the Internet.

The father of the Internet, Tim Berners-Lee.

As for who really *did* invent the Internet, that is impossible to really tie to just one person, as many scientists and researchers contributed to the technology. However, if you were to narrow it to one person, it would likely be Tim Berners-Lee, a British computer scientist who is the director of the World Wide Web Consortium (W3C) and the founder of the World Wide Web Foundation. Berners-Lee sent the first successful communication between an HTTP (hypertext transfer protocol) client and a server in late 1989. HTTP is the backbone on which the World Wide Web runs.

was born. The language of the Internet at that time was HTML, which stands for hypertext markup language, and it was first developed in 1990. Alongside HTML, another crucial piece of the Internet fell into place: the uniform resource locator (URL). Internet pages were created with HTML, and each was assigned a URL so it could be easily located.

Technically, the idea for the World Wide Web was introduced in 1989, when Tim Berners-Lee laid out a proposal for it. However, Berners-Lee didn't really start working on the Web until 1990. By late 1990, he had developed the three main technologies that launched the Internet as we know it today: HTML, HTTP, and URLs. He published the first web page in late 1990 as well.

Just three years later, the White House and the United Nations were on board with the exciting new technology—both organizations established Internet presences in 1993. Two years later, the launch of Amazon.com forever changed how people shop. Internet shopping was available before Amazon, but not on such a huge scale. Amazon changed the face of online shopping—and in the process, it managed to unseat numerous brick-and-mortar stores.

LET'S CHAT!

One feature that initially drew people to the Internet was chat rooms. These were spaces where users could log on and chat anonymously with other people with similar interests. They were wildly popular among many users, and people who tended to be shy or introverted in regular public settings often found chat rooms to be a place where they could find friends and companionship without the pressures of face-to-face interactions.

The first chat room was actually developed in the early 1970s. It was called Talkomatic, and it was created at the

Chat rooms were very popular in the early days of the Internet.

University of Illinois for academic use. However, the creators quickly found that people were more interested in the social aspect of Talkomatic than the academic side.

Talkomatic was very limited—only five people could log on at a time. In 1980, CompuServe solved this problem with the CB Simulator, which allowed more than one hundred thousand users to sign on each night. Still, Internet access was not widespread in homes until the 1990s, and during that decade, America Online (AOL), Prodigy, and Yahoo! all launched chat services.

In the early days of chat rooms, they suffered from a slightly tawdry image. People found a certain anonymous intimacy in chat rooms—because they weren't using their real names, they felt free to say things they wouldn't normally say and perhaps express some feelings they wouldn't normally share. Cyber-sex became an issue, with people forming intimate online relationships with strangers. And worse, minors and naïve adults in chat rooms were sometimes targeted by online predators, who exploited their trust.

But then businesses began to realize the usefulness of chat services for work purposes. Services such as AOL Instant Messenger, launched in 1997, allowed users to chat one-on-one with each other electronically. If you needed an immediate answer from a coworker, you could shoot them an instant message via AOL or whatever instant-messaging service your company used.

As it turned out, instant-messaging services soon overtook the popularity of chat rooms. Chat rooms died out in the late 1990s and early 2000s, but instant messaging remained for quite a while longer, only fairly recently being replaced by texting.

There has been a bit of a renaissance of chat rooms; there are several apps available for chat rooms. However, they aren't

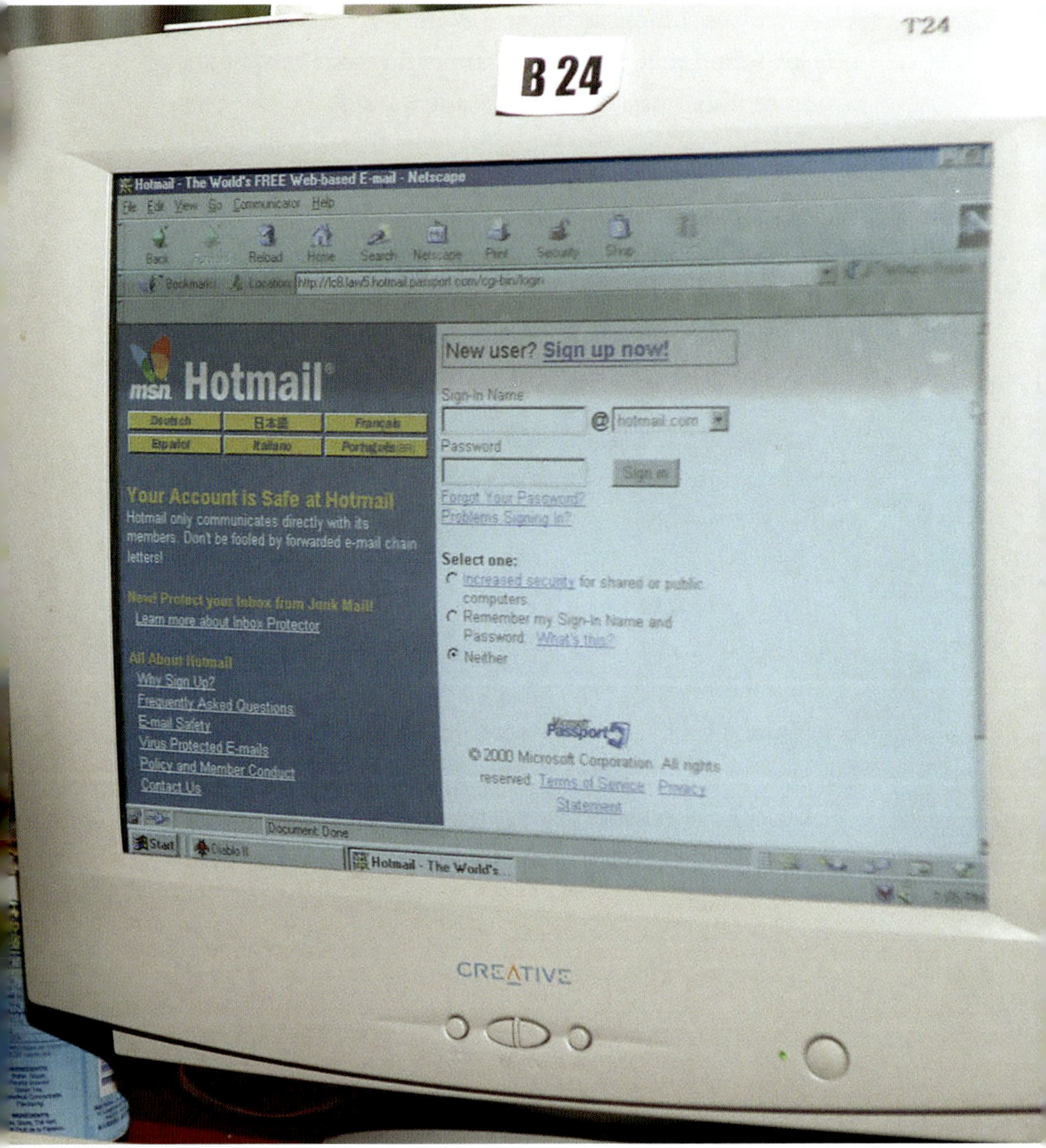

Hotmail was an early web-based e-mail interface that remains in use today.

terribly widely used anymore, with people instead using texting as their main method of communication.

SEND ME AN E-MAIL

Much like chat rooms, e-mail actually existed for quite a while before it achieved mainstream usage. The first networked e-mail is believed to have been sent in 1971, and by the 1980s, e-mail was in fairly frequent use among the military, government employees, and college students. But it didn't become popular among the general public until the 1990s, in large part because the general public didn't have much in the way of Internet access before then.

Some of the popular early e-mail services were Pegasus Mail and Eudora. But once the World Wide Web was established, web-based e-mail services became more popular. In 1996, with many Americans having Internet access either at home or on public computers, Hotmail launched the first web-based e-mail service. Accounts were free, and the popularity of the service made it an enticing buy for Microsoft, who snapped the company up for a cool $400 million in 1997. Yahoo! also

SPAM: IT'S NOT JUST A SALTY MEAT

Before 1998, Spam was just a vaguely disgusting but oddly addictive luncheon meat consisting of mostly pork products sold in small cans. But come 1998, the word took on a whole new meaning when the Oxford English Dictionary added it as a term to describe "irrelevant or inappropriate messages sent on the Internet to a large number of recipients"—in other words, unsolicited junk mail. Spam became the bane of e-mail users' existence, and virtually all e-mail programs implemented spam filters to help users filter out unwanted content.

offered a web-based e-mail service. Google's incredibly popular Gmail was a later option among web-based e-mail services.

THE RISE OF GOOGLE

If Amazon changed the face of online shopping, then Google changed the face of online searching. When the World Wide Web was launched, the ability to search on it was primitive. But in 1993, the first search engine was launched. It was known as W3Catalog, and it was developed by Oscar Nierstrasz. In the months that followed, W3Catalog was followed by Aliweb, JumpStation, Infoseek, Altavista, and Lycos, among others. In this same time period, Yahoo! launched a web directory, which was not exactly a proper search engine but was considered along the same lines.

Numerous search engines were developed and released over the next few years, but the one that would take over the vast majority of Internet searches was created in 1998: Google.

Google is *huge*. So huge, in fact, that the word "google" was added as a verb to the Oxford English Dictionary and the Merriam-Webster Collegiate Dictionary in 2006. Before Google, people used to talk about "doing an Internet search." After Google, that phrase became shortened to simply the verb "google," as in "I googled pugs to find out more about the breed."

But what made Google so popular and so widely used? Well, from a business standpoint, it offered some features that other search engines didn't. Search engine optimization (SEO) is key to businesses that have an online presence. SEO refers to how visible a website is in a search engine's results. That is, suppose you own a company that makes widgets. If someone types "widgets" into Google, where will your company show up in the results? First? Two hundredth? Google provides

The headquarters of Google, arguably the giant of the Internet, is located near San Jose, California.

suggestions and tools to help website owners achieve higher rankings in the search results.

Google Analytics is also a big draw for business owners. Google offers a robust set of analytics that allow website owners to analyze the traffic to their website, such as where their visitors are coming from. This can help business owners target their marketing. And tied in with that is Google AdWords, which allows website owners to advertise their business in Google search results.

From a business standpoint, all of these features make Google very attractive. But Google is also wildly popular among other Internet users. It's quick—the results of your search are returned within seconds. It's comprehensive—you'll get more results than you dreamed possible about pretty much any topic you can think of. It's user friendly—you can type any odd thing you can think of into the search bar and you'll get results. You wouldn't believe how many computer issues you can solve simply by googling the problem. And it has a ton of fun related applications, such as Google Maps and Google Earth (mapping and satellite image tools), Google+ (a social media presence), and Google Picasa (a place to catalog your images and create slideshows of them). And let's not forget Gmail, Google's e-mail system, where you can get a free e-mail account with robust features. For casual Internet users, Google's integrated environment is pretty much a one-stop shop. It's easy to use, it's convenient, and everything's in one place.

From a communications standpoint, Google has made a huge impact. In the nearly two decades since it was created, it has grown from a simple search engine to a full-featured communications platform. The e-mail services are widely used and reliable—users can access their e-mail at any time, from anywhere. Gmail is currently the world's largest e-mail service;

Google offers an extensive range of connected applications.

as of mid-2014, they had more than five hundred million active users. Picasa allows people to share their pictures and videos with each other. Google+ provides a social-media platform where people can share ideas, information, and media. Google Voice, one of the many Google applications, allows users to consolidate all phone numbers into one and provides voicemail services. And Google Docs allows users to create and share documents and spreadsheets online, to facilitate collaboration.

In short, Google took nearly all the ways that people communicate and tied them into one nice, neat package. Many people use tools other than Google, of course—you might have a Gmail account for e-mail but not use Google Voice for your phone services. But if you want it, nearly all of your communications tools are available in some manner through Google. And that is a large part of why Google is such a dominant force in the search engine domain.

DECADE IN REVIEW

While tensions flared with the Middle East and conflicts and wars raged in Europe and Africa, an information and communications explosion was happening in the United States. The Internet and World Wide Web were developing rapidly and bringing out new ways for people to gather information and communicate. The danger, of course, was that not all of the information was reliable, and the relative anonymity of the Internet brought about communications between people that might not otherwise have occurred—which was not always a positive thing.

But despite the dangers of this new form of communication, it was also *exciting*! Not since the invention of the telephone had communication been revolutionized in this manner. Suddenly, people had a new way to instantly connect and communicate, and they loved it. Plus, the Internet opened up a whole new world of "friends." And that new world would only be furthered when social media came on the scene in the next decade.

SIX

2000s: Turmoil and Change

ALL OF THE TECHNOLOGICAL CHANGES happening in the previous decades were exciting, but it also brought about fear in the form of Y2K. The term was an abbreviation for "the year 2000," and it was used to describe the fear that the exact moment when 1999 turned into 2000 would result in utter technological chaos.

The problem was that computers generally used the last two digits of a year to determine the date—just like we say '99 when referring to the year 1999, so do computers. There was widespread fear that when the year became '00, computers would interpret it as 1900, rather than 2000. By this point, computers had pretty much become the backbone of society—nearly everything ran on computers. So if the computers got confused by the date, what would happen? Would the technology that powered our very civilization simply shut down at that very second?

As it turned out, fears about Y2K were mostly unfounded. The majority of corporations and entities simply addressed the problem by upgrading their systems so that computers

could recognize the year 2000. And so began a new decade, a new century, and a whole new millennium.

Fears about Y2K weren't the only thing making Americans uneasy at the turn of the millennium, though. Tensions in the Middle East weren't resolved, and on a sunny morning on September 11, 2001, Americans' fears about the threat in the Middle East were realized. At 8:46 a.m. EST, American Airlines Flight 11 crashed into the north tower of the World Trade Center in New York City. Air-traffic controllers knew the flight had been hijacked before it crashed because the hijackers' announcements to passengers on the flight were transmitted to the control tower. But to the general public, it first appeared to be just an incredibly tragic accident.

That is, until 9:03 a.m. EST, when United Airlines Flight 175 crashed into the south tower of the World Trade Center. And then 9:37 a.m. EST, when American Airlines Flight 77 crashed into the Pentagon near Washington, DC. And then 10:03 a.m. EST, when United Airlines Flight 93 crashed into a field near Shanksville, Pennsylvania, the passengers on the flight believed to have overtaken the hijackers in a desperate attempt to save the flight. It is assumed that the hijackers' intended target for this flight was either the White House or the Capitol building in Washington, DC.

The 9/11 attacks were the largest terrorist attacks on US soil, with nearly three thousand lives lost in the attacks. President George W. Bush responded quickly and forcefully, initiating the War on Terror against al-Qaeda, whose founder, Osama bin Laden, masterminded the attacks. The War on Terror officially went on until May 23, 2013, when President Barack Obama declared it over and called the troops home.

***Opposite*: The terrorist attacks of 9/11 devastated the nation.**

The War on Terror was in the forefront of Americans' minds in the 2000s, but it wasn't the only concern. In August 2005, New Orleans and the coastal cities on the Gulf of Mexico were devastated by Hurricane Katrina, a Category 5 storm that claimed more than one thousand lives and caused roughly $108 billion in property damage, making it the costliest natural disaster in United States history.

Residents of New Orleans slogged through deep water that flooded the city after levees broke under the force of Hurricane Katrina.

Katrina wasn't only costly; it was also controversial. Many Americans questioned the response and relief efforts of government agencies and officials, such as the Federal Emergency Management Agency (FEMA), the New Orleans Police Department, and even President George W. Bush.

If President Bush had stepped into a minefield when he took office in 2001, just eight months before the 9/11 attacks, President Barack Obama stepped into a similar minefield when he took office in 2009. The election of Barack Obama to the presidency was monumental because he became the first African American to hold the office of president. But more than that, Americans wanted change, and Obama promised that. In 2007, the United States had entered into a financial crisis that was still going strong when Obama took office in 2009. The real estate market had crashed, leaving millions of Americans paying mortgages on homes that were worth maybe half of what they had bought them for. Unemployment rates were high, having not particularly recovered from the dot-com bust in the early 2000s when the phenomenal growth of Internet companies suddenly came to a crashing halt. In short, America was at war, facing rampant unemployment, and looking at a crashed housing market. Times were bleak, with many people likening the situation to the Great Depression of the 1930s.

And so, it was an exciting time when a new president took office and promised change—promised to clean up the messes that many felt the previous president had left behind. Whether that change actually happened … well, that depends on whom you ask. Some Americans feel that President Obama made things worse, while others think he did as much as he could while being blocked at every turn by a Republican Congress. One thing's for certain, though:

a new communications medium gave Americans a very large platform on which to voice their opinions!

SOCIAL MEDIA: NOT ALWAYS SO SOCIABLE

The Internet became a place of social interaction when chat rooms were developed in the 1980s and 1990s, and in 1997, a website called Six Degrees launched. It is believed to be the first social media site—a space where people could create a profile and become friends with other users. Chat rooms were a bit different because the relationships existed only while both users were in the chat room; with a social media site, the user's profile is always there, and the connections he or she makes remain even when the user and others aren't logged on to the site.

But again, not everyone had Internet access in 1997, so Six Degrees wasn't all that widely used. By the 2000s, though, many more people had access to the Internet—the History Cooperative estimates about one hundred million people by the year 2000, in fact. And in 2003, the first widely used social media platform was launched: MySpace.

On MySpace, users would create a profile, add friends, and share likes and dislikes, as well as pictures, videos, and music clips. Sounds a lot like Facebook, right? That's because it was—MySpace was a precursor of Facebook.

MySpace is still around today, but it's used primarily by musicians and those in the music industry. For whatever reason, it has retained its popularity in that circle, even though most other MySpace users have moved on to other social media sites, such as Facebook, Twitter, Instagram, and Tumblr.

Facebook was actually created just a year after MySpace launched. A Harvard University student named Mark Zuckerberg created it for Harvard students. It was wildly popular, and Zuckerberg released it shortly thereafter to the rest of the world. He admitted to be rather surprised at the success of his fun little project, which he created rather on a whim: "Well, it's funny. When I was getting started, with my roommates in college, you never think that you could build this company or anything like that, right? Because, I mean, we were college students, right? And we were just building stuff 'cause we thought it was cool." At the time, Zuckerberg and his friends had no idea that their new communication tool would have such an impact on the Internet and social media.

Back in the early days of Facebook, you could do silly things like poke your friends or throw a chicken at them (virtually, of course!). But now Facebook is far more robust. It allows users to post status updates of any length (type in whatever you want to say, and all your friends can read it), pictures and videos, links to other media (such as news stories), and so on. Many people even use Facebook as a marketing tool for businesses, and there are countless Facebook groups created for users with common interests. More than one billion people use Facebook, and as a result, Zuckerberg is now one very, very wealthy individual!

Twitter came along in 2006 and currently has more than five hundred million users. Like MySpace and Facebook, Twitter allows users to build networks of friends and then share their thoughts. The difference is that Twitter only allows users to post messages of 140 characters or less. So, much like a text message, a tweet is very succinct!

Another popular social media platform is Instagram, which was created in 2010. Like MySpace, Facebook, and Twitter, Instagram involves creating a network of friends. However, it is limited to photo and video sharing; users can upload a photo or a short video clip and share it with their followers.

Social media platforms are available as apps for smartphones, so users never have to be away from their social media accounts.

Instagram also offers some photo-editing tools so users can create some neat effects on their photos before sharing them. The site now boasts more than three hundred million users.

There are many other social media sites, such as Snapchat and Vine, and they generally work in a similar manner—users set up a profile and a network of friends, and they socialize via the platform. It's easy and it's fun. However, there is a potentially negative side to this sort of online social networking. The Internet gives users a feeling of relative anonymity. Sure, on many sites you have a profile and you are linked to people you know, but you also have a level of protection in that you aren't saying anything face to face with others—instead, you're putting your thoughts out there while hiding behind a computer or phone screen, a relatively safe place. And this sort of environment has led to a lot of conflict on the Internet—people sometimes feel free to say things they wouldn't normally say in polite company, which naturally creates some tension and conflict.

This made the 2012 presidential elections particularly heated among Americans. The same was true in 2008, but social media was in its infancy and not nearly as widely used. By

The Rise of the #Hashtag

Twitter was the first social media platform to make widespread use of the pound symbol (#) as a "hashtag." These symbols are placed in front of a word with no spaces, like #summervacation, to categorize a tweet as part of a larger group or conversation. When a user clicks on the hashtagged word, they are connected to other tweets on the same topic. The idea was first proposed in 2007 by Chris Messina, a Google employee who sent the first tweet to use a hashtag: "how do you feel about using # (pound) for groups. As in #barcamp [msg]?" Today, widely used hashtags stand out as trending. These are determined by a computer **algorithm** that recognizes a specific hashtag's popularity. Soon, hashtags caught on with other platforms like Facebook, Instagram, and Pinterest. By 2014, it had become clear that hashtags were here to stay; that year the Oxford English and Merriam-Webster dictionaries first recognized and listed "hashtag" as an official word.

2012, it was everywhere—and people wasted no time in sharing their strong opinions on it. There is always disagreement about politics—in fact, there's an old saying that people should never discuss politics or religion in polite company for that very reason. But social media brought disagreements into the forefront and exposed the ugly side of people's natures. While some users maintained a respectful attitude about others' beliefs, many did not, and social media exploded with angry comments about the presidential candidates and their suitability for the job.

The other tricky part of social media is that it's relatively unpoliced. There are safeguards in place to try to discourage pornography and inappropriate content, but there's nothing in place to stop people from posting fake or misleading information or articles. And so, particularly with regard to politics and current events, there are generally *lots* of people posting inflammatory information that may or may not be true—and plenty of gullible people believing it without fact checking. It creates a rather dangerous cycle of fear and overreaction.

When done well, social media is an amazing communications tool. People can meet new friends from all over the world—people with similar interests and ideas, or simply people who they connect with on a personal level. And old friends and family who are separated geographically can keep in touch with each other on a daily basis. But when heated tempers and misinformation get in the way, social media can also be a platform for negativity and unease.

ENTERING THE BLOGOSPHERE

Blogging is a type of communication related to social media. The word blog stands for "weblog," and a blog is essentially an online diary of sorts that is usually shared with the general

As blogging platforms became more widely available, personal blogs sprang up everywhere.

public or a select group of readers. Many blog sites allow readers to post comments, which allows two-way communication between the blogger and his or her readers. But in general, blogging is more like an author writing his or her thoughts and readers perusing them, whereas social media tends to be more a back-and-forth conversation.

The first blog was actually written in 1994 by a student at Swarthmore College. And the term "weblog" came about in 1997. However, blogging didn't become really popular until the 2000s, when platforms such as Blogger, WordPress, and Tumblr came about. Many blogging platforms are free to use, so once Americans became aware of and interested in blogs, more and more people started creating their own. As of early 2005, it was reported that more than 10 percent of Americans read blogs. And they were beginning to gain more credibility as well. Blogger Garrett M. Graff, for example, was given White House press credentials, and politicians and news services began to use blogs. *Huffington Post*, for example, a fairly popular news outlet among liberal Americans, features a lot of blogs.

Blogs can be a powerful communications tool—and not just for the news media. Everyday people with knowledge in particular areas can choose to share their knowledge via a blog—and others searching for information may find it in a blog when they can't find it elsewhere. Blogs can be a way of connection, too. For example, there are a lot of "mommy blogs" out there, written by women who are raising children. Other mothers who are at a similar stage in life find commonalities and connections by following these blogs.

Even on lighter topics, there are blogs for everything. For example, there's a blog written by a teenager who reviews the restaurants in his local area. Every Sunday he dines out with his father at a different restaurant, and then he writes a review of it. He has gained quite a following among people who enjoy reading his food reviews.

So even though blogs are mostly a one-way street in terms of communication, they are still an important communications medium for people in the twenty-first century. They may not be as interactive as a social media site, but they have no less to say.

THE RISE OF SMARTPHONES

Blogs and social media became infinitely more popular when they were suddenly available on the go via a little invention called the smartphone. Smartphones, which were essentially mobile phones with simple computing abilities built in, were

The first smartphones weren't quite as sleek as the models today, but they were equally useful.

conceived of back in the mid-1970s, and the first ones were invented in the 1990s, but they were few and far between—and very expensive!

In the 2000s, though, the technology developed and became more affordable, and more people began to use smartphones. Phones using the Palm OS and BlackBerry OS (operating system) were popular in the early 2000s, along with PocketPC (later known as Windows Mobile) technology.

These phones allowed users to send and receive e-mail, surf the Web, and even fax things. Some required a **stylus**, which users would tap on the screen, and many incorporated small keyboards that enabled users to compose text messages much more easily.

The smartphone industry got a major push forward by an unsurprising source: Apple Computer, or Apple Inc. as it came to be known. Always on the cutting edge of innovation and creativity, Apple introduced the sleek iPhone in 2007. The iPhone did basically the same things that other smartphones did, but it looked much more elegant because it didn't have a clunky keyboard attached. Rather, it used a touchscreen interface that actually *worked*. (People had been playing around with touchscreen technology for years, but it wasn't terribly accurate. The iPhone changed that.)

Whereas the BlackBerry and Palm devices had been designed with business productivity in mind, the iPhone was designed more for fun. It had all the business functionality of its competitors, but it was also fun and user friendly—much like Apple's Mac had been a fun, user-friendly alternative to the more serious-minded PCs.

Opposite: The Apple iPhone 6 Plus.

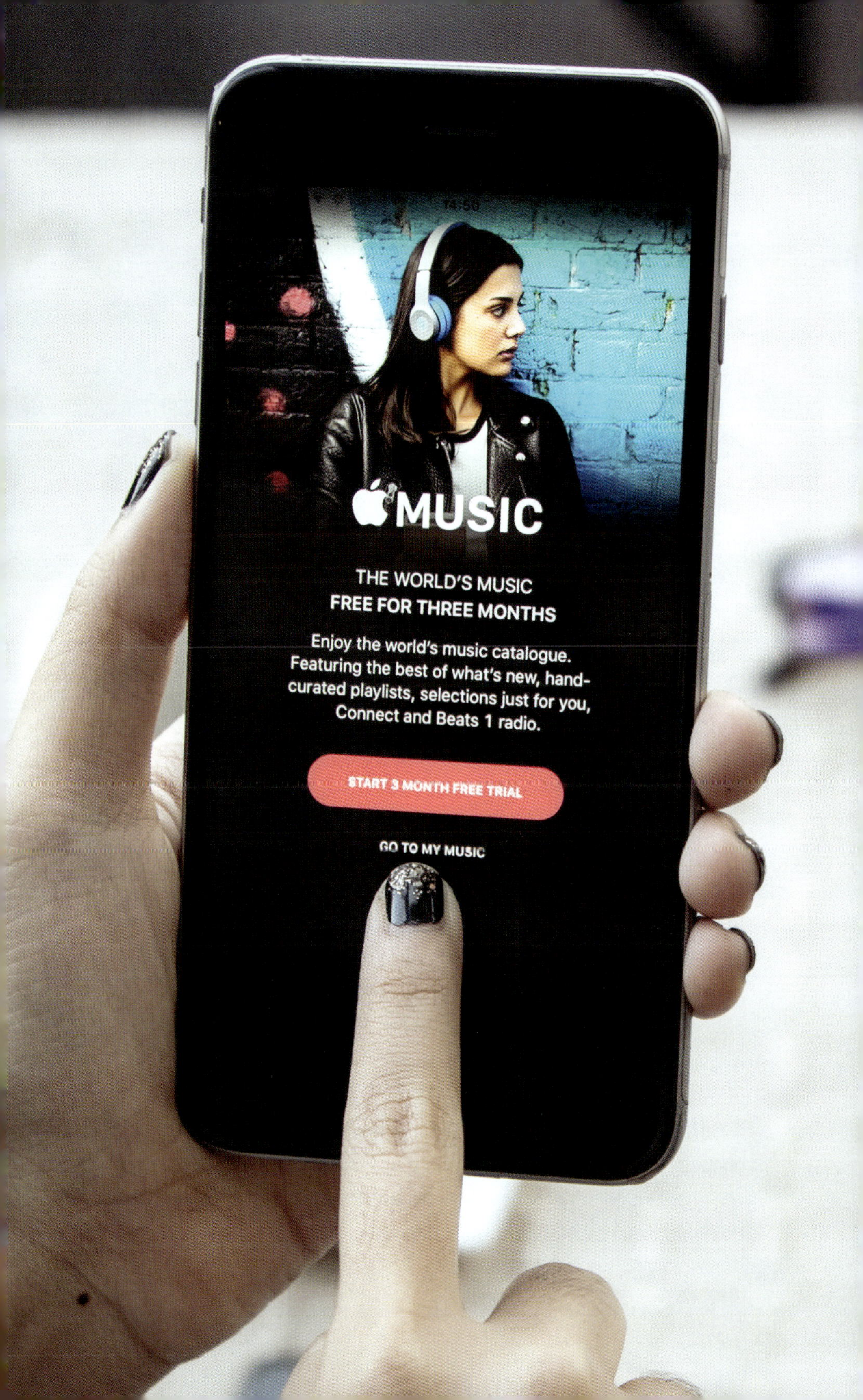
MUSIC
THE WORLD'S MUSIC
FREE FOR THREE MONTHS
Enjoy the world's music catalogue. Featuring the best of what's new, hand-curated playlists, selections just for you, Connect and Beats 1 radio.
START 3 MONTH FREE TRIAL
GO TO MY MUSIC

Text Me!

Texting is everywhere now! It's estimated that in 2015, 8.3 trillion text messages were sent. Yes, *trillion!* And on today's smartphones, it's so simple. But it wasn't always so easy …

When the technology for texting was first developed back in the early 1990s, the majority of cell phones didn't have keyboards; they only had the standard telephone number pad with the letters on each number. So, for example, the letter *S* was found on the 7 key. But it was the fourth letter on the 7 key (the key contained PQRS). So if you wanted to type an *S* in a text message, you had to press the 7 key four times to get an *S* to appear. And if you accidentally hit it five times … well, you were scrolled right back to the *P*. Or another character, if there were other characters covered by that key as well. In short, it was a real pain to type out text messages.

Texting charges often applied. While unlimited texting plans are fairly common today, when texting was first invented, many people had to pay for text messages.

Nowadays, though, texting is incredibly simple and often free. And so it has become a major method of communication for people around the globe. Whereas you used to have to call someone to talk to them, you can now send a quick text. That generally means you're more likely to get a response—there are certain occasions (business meetings, for example) where a person wouldn't be able to take a phone call but might be able to answer a quick text message. This ease and accessibility has made texting an extremely powerful method of communication now.

There are, of course, downsides. For example, there's a certain etiquette that goes along with texting. It's not polite to text when you're on a date or perhaps enjoying a meal with friends or family. Doing so can certainly annoy the people around you, who rightfully

Texting is easy, but the etiquette can be tricky.

feel ignored when their companion pays more attention to a phone screen than to them!

Further, it can be hard to discern tone in a text message (or an e-mail, for that matter). When you talk face to face or even on the phone with a person, you have certain variations in your voice tone and a general body language that helps convey your meaning. Texting and e-mail don't allow any of that, so something you intend to be a joke may not be perceived as such when the person on the receiving end can't see your body language or hear your tone of voice. There have certainly been many miscommunications via text and e-mail when recipients have misunderstood a sender's tone!

But that's what emoticons are for, right? Add a little smiley face, and the recipient will know you're joking. Well … not always. They do help, certainly, but sometimes the recipient will think you're deliberately mocking them if you send a smiley face!

So by all means text and enjoy its ease as a communication tool, but be aware of the limitations in communication and of texting etiquette!

Shortly after the launch of the iPhone, Apple also launched its App Store, which made the iPhone all the more enticing. Other smartphones had used apps (short for "applications") as well, but they were often somewhat difficult to use and not as full featured as the full version of a product. The apps designed for the iPhone, on the other hand, were robust, usable, and perhaps most importantly, designed specifically for the very small interface of a phone. No more scrolling sideways to try to see features on the edges of an application; the iPhone's apps were all perfectly sized for the screen.

And the apps were endless—people developed more and more of them, and soon there was a saying that "there's an app for that!" because in truth, there pretty much *was* an app for everything!

Nowadays the Android is the main competitor to the iPhone, and their features and interfaces are often very similar.

Android phones are major competitors to iPhones.

People often choose which smartphone to buy based solely on price (iPhones are not cheap!) and their allegiance to a particular manufacturer (Apple fans are a devoted customer base). And as communications tools, smartphones are developing with new features pretty much on a daily basis. Maybe soon they'll be driving our cars for us?

WHAT THE FUTURE HOLDS

It's anyone's guess what the future holds in terms of communication. While families in the 1950s were excited by dedicated, individual phone lines and touch-tone dialing, they likely would never have dreamed that in half a century or so, they could hold in their hands a mobile, cordless phone that was also a tiny computer on which they could manage virtually every aspect of their daily lives. It's almost impossible to comprehend, isn't it?

One thing's for certain: the future of communication will not be boring. Researchers will continue to find ways to astonish and entice us with new communications tools.

Notes

CHAPTER 1:

p. 11, "We are interested … espionage agent." Interview with J. Edgar Hoover, originally published August 11, 1950 in *U.S. News & World Report*. http://www.usnews.com/news/national/articles/2008/05/16/how-communists-operate-an-interview-with-j-edgar.

p. 13, "His proposition is … in this country." News broadcast by Edward R. Murrow, delivered on April 13, 1954. http://www.americanrhetoric.com/speeches/edwardrmurrowtomccarthy.htm.

CHAPTER 3:

p. 35, "I am not a crook." Press Q&A with President Richard M. Nixon on November 7, 1973. http://www.emersonkent.com/speeches/i_am_not_a_crook.htm.

p. 35, "I want the facts out … telling the truth." Press Q&A with President Richard M. Nixon on November 7, 1973. http://www.emersonkent.com/speeches/i_am_not_a_crook.htm.

CHAPTER 4:

p. 57, "Hello, I'm Macintosh … you can't lift." 1984 Apple Macintosh launch video. http://www.ibtimes.com/steve-jobs-landmark-1984-apple-macintosh-launch-video-321860.

CHAPTER 5:

p. 66, "took the … Internet." Al Gore in an interview on CNN's *Late Edition with Wolf Blitzer*, March 9, 1999.

CHAPTER 6:

p. 83, "Well, it's funny … it was cool." Lesley Stahl interview with Mark Zuckerberg for *60 Minutes*. http://www.cbsnews.com/news/mark-zuckerberg-and-facebook-whats-next/.

p. 85, "how do … [msg]?" Twitter post by Chris Messina, August 23, 2007. https://twitter.com/chrismessina/status/223115412?ref_src=twsrc%5Etfw.

Glossary

algorithm A step-by-step process for solving a problem, often used by a computer.

blacklist A group of people viewed negatively or with suspicion.

carbon paper Thin paper coated with carbon "ink" that, when placed between two sheets of paper, can make a copy of what is then written or typed on the top piece of paper.

Cold War An era of political tension and hostility between the United States and its allies and the Soviet Union and its allies, usually thought to have lasted from about 1945 until 1990.

communism A political system in which all property is collectively owned and society is essentially free from classes.

counterculture Describing an attitude or lifestyle that differs from mainstream society.

extremist group A group—usually political and/or religious in nature—that resorts to extreme measures to try to get others to conform to their way of thinking.

feminism The belief that women's rights should be equal to men's in political, social, and economic matters.

genocide The systematic killing of a group of people, often for reasons based on politics, religion, or ethnicity.

Great Depression A massive economic downturn in the United States lasting from roughly 1929 to 1939.

hieroglyph A picture that represents a word or sound, often found in ancient Egyptian writings.

hippie A member of the counterculture who appeared unconventional in his or her dress and grooming and was often associated with drug culture and a rejection of long-held societal values.

immunodeficiency disease A disease that lowers the body's immune system.

Islamism Based on the Islamic religion, Islamism is a political movement that encourages a fundamental return to the early tenets of Islam.

mnemonic Relating to memory.

nomadic Wandering, traveling, without a permanent home.

patriarchal Describing a society controlled by males.

photojournalism A practice of using photography to convey news and current events.

protocol A plan or set of instructions.

sitcom Short for "situation comedy," a genre of television show.

stylus A pen-like device used to write on a device such as a smartphone or tablet.

suburb The outlying, largely residential, part of a city.

taboo Describing something that is not widely accepted.

telephone exchange A central system that connects multiple phone lines.

teletypewriter A device consisting of a keyboard, a printer, and a transmitter that allows people to transmit and received typed messages.

Further Information

BOOKS

Blum, Andrew. *Tubes: A Journey to the Center of the Internet.* New York: Ecco, 2013.

Hilmes, Michelle. *Only Connect: A Cultural History of Broadcasting in the United States.* Boston, MA: Wadsworth Publishing, 2013.

Lapsley, Phil. *Exploding the Phone.* New York: Grove Press, 2014.

Lotz, Amanda D. *The Television Will Be Revolutionized.* New York: NYU Press, 2014.

Ryan, Johnny. *A History of the Internet and the Digital Future.* London: Reaktion Books, 2013.

FILMS

The Social Network. Sony Pictures, 2010.

WEBSITES

History Channel: Invention of the PC

www.history.com/topics/inventions/invention-of-the-pc

The History Channel's website provides an in-depth article on the invention of the PC and the birth of the computer age.

The National Museum of American History: Communications

americanhistory.si.edu/collections/subjects/communications

Explore over seven thousand items that chart the history of communications in the United States in the National Museum's collection.

Telephony Museum

www.telephonymuseum.com

This site contains a lot of interesting and useful information about the history of the telephone and its development.

Bibliography

Abramson, Albert. *The History of Television, 1942 to 2000.* Jefferson, NC: McFarland & Company, 2003.

Adams, Mark, and Jeff Parsons. "Matti Makkonen Dead: Text Message Inventor Dies Aged 63." Mirror Online, July 2, 2015. http://www.mirror.co.uk/news/technology-science/technology/matti-makkonen-dead-text-message-5986214.

"The Bay of Pigs." John F. Kennedy Presidential Library and Museum. http://www.jfklibrary.org/JFK/JFK-in-History/The-Bay-of-Pigs.aspx.

"A Brief History of Slide Projectors." Kodak.com. http://www.kodak.com/eknec/documents/a6/0900688a807890a6/history.pdf.

"The Cell Phone Timeline." Interactive Media Lab at the University of Florida. http://iml.jou.ufl.edu/projects/fall04/keith/history1.htm.

Coopersmith, Jonathan. *Faxed: The Rise and Fall of the Fax Machine.* Baltimore, MD: Johns Hopkins University Press, 2015.

Covert, Adrian. "Gmail at 10: How Google Dominated E-Mail." CNN Money, April 1, 2014. http://money.cnn.com/2014/04/01/technology/gmail/.

"Cuban Missile Crisis." John F. Kennedy Presidential Library and Museum. http://www.jfklibrary.org/JFK/JFK-in-History/Cuban-Missile-Crisis.aspx.

Cumo, Christopher. *Science and Technology in 20th-Century American Life.* Westport, CT: Greenwood Press, 2007.

Dewey, Caitlin. "A Complete History of the Rise and Fall—and Reincarnation!—of the Beloved '90s Chatroom." *Washington*

Post, October 30, 2014. https://www.washingtonpost.com/news/the-intersect/wp/2014/10/30/a-complete-history-of-the-rise-and-fall-and-reincarnation-of-the-beloved-90s-chatroom/.

Donnelly, Dave, Greg Park, Ludwig Reimmer, and Grace Wood. "The Decline of Pager Technology." Dartmouth University. http://faculty.tuck.dartmouth.edu/images/uploads/faculty/ron-adner/Pagers.pdf.

"Edward R. Murrow." Biography.com. http://www.biography.com/people/edward-r-murrow-9419104#final-years-and-legacy.

"Edward R. Murrow: Response to Senator Joe McCarthy on CBS' *See It Now*." American Rhetoric Online Speech Bank. http://www.americanrhetoric.com/speeches/edwardrmurrowtomccarthy.htm.

Fleishman, Glenn. "Timeline: A Brief History of Email." Macworld. http://www.macworld.com/article/1167303/timeline_a_brief_history_of_email.html.

Garber, Megan. "Our Numbered Days: The Evolution of the Area Code." The *Atlantic*, February 13, 2014. http://www.theatlantic.com/technology/archive/2014/02/our-numbered-days-the-evolution-of-the-area-code/283803/.

Haralovich, Mary Beth, and Lauren Rabinovitz, eds. *Television, History, and American Culture: Feminist Critical Essays*. Durham, NC: Duke University Press, 1999.

"The History of Answering Machines." Federal Communications Commission. https://transition.fcc.gov/cgb/kidszone/history_ans_machine.html.

"History of the Internet." New Media Institute. http://www.newmedia.org/history-of-the-internet.html?page=4.

"The History of the Mobile Phone." *Washington Post*, September 9, 2014. https://www.washingtonpost.com/news/the-switch/wp/2014/09/09/the-history-of-the-mobile-phone/.

"The History of Social Media." History Cooperative. http://historycooperative.org/the-history-of-social-media/.

"History of the Web." World Wide Web Foundation. http://webfoundation.org/about/vision/history-of-the-web/.

"How Communists Operate: An Interview with J. Edgar Hoover." *U.S. News & World Report*, May 16, 2008. http://www.usnews.com/news/national/articles/2008/05/16/how-communists-operate-an-interview-with-j-edgar.

"How Cordless and Cell Phones Work." The Telecommunications History Group. http://www.telcomhistory.org/vm/scienceCellPhones.shtml.

"I Am Not a Crook." Press Q&A with President Richard M. Nixon on November 7, 1973. EmersonKent.com. http://www.emersonkent.com/speeches/i_am_not_a_crook.htm.

"Internet History of the 1980s." Computer History Museum. http://www.computerhistory.org/internethistory/1980s/.

Jordan, Winthrop, Miriam Greenblatt, and John S. Bowes. *The Americans: A History*. Boston: McDougal Littell, 1996.

Leiner, Barry M., et al. "Brief History of the Internet." Internet Society. http://www.internetsociety.org/internet/what-internet/history-internet/brief-history-internet.

Lievrouw, Leah A., and Sonia Livingstone, eds. *The Handbook of New Media*. London: Sage Publications, 2006.

"Mark Zuckerberg and Facebook: What's Next?" *60 Minutes*. http://www.cbsnews.com/news/mark-zuckerberg-and-facebook-whats-next/.

Mathur, Aditi. "A Steve Jobs Landmark: The 1984 Apple Macintosh Launch Video." *International Business Times*. October 7, 2011. http://www.ibtimes.com/steve-jobs-landmark-1984-apple-macintosh-launch-video-321860.

"Motorola DynaTAC Series." Vintage Mobile Phones. http://www.vintagemobilephones.com/motorola_dynatac_series.html.

O'Connell, Kate. "Happy Birthday, Copy Machine! Happy Birthday, Copy Machine!" NPR, October 23, 2013. http://www.npr.org/2013/10/23/239241106/happy-birthday-copy-machine-happy-birthday-copy-machine.

Ray, Amanda. "This History and Evolution of Cell Phones." Art Institutes. https://www.artinstitutes.edu/blog/the-history-and-evolution-of-cell-phones.

Ryan, Johnny. *A History of the Internet and the Digital Future*. London: Reaktion Books, 2010.

Shahi, Gurinder, and Joseph Greco. *Financing Technology Innovation*. CSEM and GBI Books, 2008.

Spigel, Lynn. "Family on Television." Museum of Broadcast Communications. http://www.museum.tv/eotv/familyontel.htm.

Thompson, Robert J. "Television in the United States." Encyclopedia Britannica. http://www.britannica.com/art/television-in-the-United-States.

"Timeline of HIV/AIDS." AIDS.gov. https://www.aids.gov/hiv-aids-basics/hiv-aids-101/aids-timeline/.

Vare, Ethlie Ann, and Greg Ptacek. *Patently Female: From AZT to TV Dinners, Stories of Women Inventors and Their Breakthrough Ideas*. Hoboken, NJ: John Wiley & Sons, 2001.

Index

Page numbers in **boldface** are illustrations. Entries in **boldface** are glossary terms.

About the Author

CATHLEEN SMALL is an author and editor who has written numerous books for Cavendish Square Publishing. A voracious reader, Cathleen has a keen interest in pop culture, particularly from the 1980s to the present. Cathleen lives in the San Francisco Bay Area with her two young sons and too many animals.